TOEFL®
VOCABULARY
PREP

KAPLAN

PUBLISHING

New York

ACKNOWLEDGMENTS

Special thanks to the team that made this book possible:

Kim Bowers, Lola Dart, Alexis Ferreri, Joanna Graham, Allison Harm, Richard J. Lapierre, Shmuel Ross, and many others who have contributed materials and advice over the years.

TOEFL® is a registered trademark of the Educational Testing Service, which neither sponsors nor endorses this product.

This publication is designed to provide accurate information in regard to the subject matter covered as of its publication date, with the understanding that knowledge and best practice constantly evolve. The publisher is not engaged in rendering medical, legal, accounting, or other professional service. If medical or legal advice or other expert assistance is required, the services of a competent professional should be sought. This publication is not intended for use in clinical practice or the delivery of medical care. To the fullest extent of the law, neither the Publisher nor the Editors assume any liability for any injury and/or damage to persons or property arising out of or related to any use of the material contained in this book.

Published by Kaplan Publishing, a division of Kaplan, Inc.
750 Third Avenue
New York, NY 10017

Printed in the United States of America

10 9 8 7 6 5 4 3 2 1

ISBN: 978-1-62523-340-0

Kaplan Publishing print books are available at special quantity discounts to use for sales promotions, employee premiums, or educational purposes. For more information or to purchase books, please call the Simon & Schuster special sales department at 866-506-1949.

FEB 0 4 2016   14.99

TABLE OF CONTENTS

Section I: Vocabulary

Section 2: Idioms

Section 3: Exercises

Section 4: Answers

HOW TO USE THIS BOOK

The Test of English as a Foreign Language is a standardized test designed to measure your ability to understand and use English as it is used in a North American university setting. Recent changes to the TOEFL have shifted its focus from how much you know about English to how well you comprehend, speak, and write English.

Whether you are taking the TOEFL iBT, TOEFL CBT, or TOEFL Pencil-and-Paper, Kaplan's TOEFL Vocabulary and Idiom Book is perfectly designed to help you learn more than 500 important TOEFL vocabulary words. Simply read the vocabulary word and its part of speech on the front of a page to determine whether you know it. On the reverse side, its definition and a sample sentence are offered to be sure that you understand the word's meaning and its correct usage.

These sample sentences are followed by the corresponding noun, verb, adjective, or adverb forms. Thus you may learn four or more new words with each entry and increase your grasp of English grammar as well as your vocabulary.

You will notice that the words are not alphabetical or grouped by category. This is to help you focus on each individual word, its meaning, and its context. Words listed alphabetically are harder to distinguish and learn because they look and sound alike. Words grouped by category are easier to guess the meaning of without truly learning their meanings.

An idiom is a word or phrase that has a special meaning apart from its literal translation—it is usually a metaphor. Only people who are good at speaking English will know what an idiom means. Idioms can be difficult to learn, and they require time and patience to master well. With this book, you will learn more than 400 important idioms. Read the idiom on the front of the page to determine whether you know it; on the reverse side, its definition and a sample sentence are offered to be sure that you understand its correct usage.

You will also see some notes in square brackets [ ]. These provide additional information about the origins of the idiom that should make it easier to memorize. In some cases—mainly with verb phrases—some words are interchangeable. In such situations, two example sentences are provided, one for each version. The most common version appears on the first page.

Study the words and idioms in any order and start on any page.

Good luck!

illustrate
illustrating, illustrated
verb

---

eligible
adjective

---

accept
accepting, accepted
verb

---

revolve
revolving, revolved
verb

---

pose
posing, posed
verb

1. to give an example of
2. to draw
1. He *illustrated* his point by showing how easy the blender was to take apart.
2. When she was done writing the book, she hired someone to *illustrate* it.
adj. illustratable; n. illustration

---

able to participate; qualified
Before you enter the contest, check all of the rules to make sure you are *eligible*.
n. eligibility

---

1. to agree
2. to receive
He *accepted* the company's proposal for the new building because it was the cheapest bid.
Please *accept* any packages that come for me while I am out of town.
adj. acceptable; n. acceptance

---

to rotate; to move in a circular motion
The moon *revolves* around the earth.
n. revolution

---

to present an attitude, position, or stance
At the council meeting tonight, I will *pose* the potential new dog park to the group.
n. pose

excavate
excavating, excavated
verb

---

tentative
adjective

---

abandon
abandoning, abandoned
verb

---

trigger
triggering, triggered
verb

---

volunteer
volunteering, volunteered
verb

to make a hole by removing something
*They plan to **excavate** the ancient ruins to learn more about the society.*
adj. excavated; n. excavation, excavator

---

unsure; undecided
*Because I don't know whether or not I will work on Sunday, I made **tentative** plans with my brother.*
adv. tentatively; n. tentativeness

---

to leave or forsake
*She is not allowed to **abandon** her post until the next officer arrives for duty.*
n. abandonment, abandoner; adj. abandoned

---

to cause (something) to happen; to set off
*A skier on the west side of the mountain **triggered** an avalanche of cascading snow.*
n. trigger

---

to offer to do something, usually without being asked, pressured, or paid
*When their babysitter canceled at the last minute, I was happy to **volunteer** to take care of their son.*
n. volunteer; adj. voluntary; adv. voluntarily

predict
predicting, predicted
verb

---

accompany
accompanying, accompanied
verb

---

relax
relaxing, relaxed
verb

---

approve
approving, approved
verb

---

restrict
restricting, restricted
verb

to state what will happen in the future; to foresee
*Gamblers try to **predict** which horse will win a race.*
n. prediction, predictability; adj. predictable; adv. predictably

---

to go or come along with
*The secretary of state **accompanied** the president on his trip.*
n. accompaniment

---

to become less tense; to slacken
*A massage will help your muscles **relax**.*
n. relaxation; adj. relaxing, relaxed

---

1. to consent to, to allow, or to endorse
2. to believe to be correct or good
*The treasurer has to **approve** all expenses.*
*His parents don't **approve** of his career choice.*
n. approval; adj. approving; adv. approvingly

---

to limit; to reduce
*Laws **restrict** the amount of tobacco a person can bring into the country.*
n. restriction; adj. restrictive; adv. restrictively

violate

violating, violated
verb

deny

denying, denied
verb

immigrate

immigrating, immigrated
verb

conform

conforming, conformed
verb

acknowledge

acknowledging, acknowledged
verb

to defy; to disobey
*Speaking to the press will **violate** the contract.*
n. violation

---

1. to dispute the truth of (a statement or fact)
2. to reject or refuse (a request)
*Her son **denied** that he had dented the car.*
*They **denied** our request for an extension.*
n. denial; adj. deniable

---

to move to a new country
*Approximately one million people **immigrate** to the United States each year.*
n. immigration, immigrant

---

1. to follow rules or standards
2. to follow social conventions to fit in
*Your new refrigerator should **conform** to energy efficiency standards.*
*Unlike his free-spirited, artistic sister, he has always tried to **conform**.*
n. conformity, conformist; adj. conformist

---

to admit or accept as a fact; to recognize
*You should **acknowledge** that your mistakes caused the accident.*
n. acknowledgment; adj. acknowledged

adhere
adhering, adhered
verb

---

degree
noun

---

audible
adjective

---

unite
uniting, united
verb

---

train
training, trained
verb

to follow; to stick to
*While running the club, the officers **adhered** to strict guidelines.*
n. adherer, adherence

1. extent
2. certification received upon graduation
*1. She understood the material to a **degree**.*
*2. He hopes to receive his **degree** next fall.*
adj. degreed, degreeless

able to be heard
*The music was barely **audible** over the child crying in the front row.*
adv. audibly; n. audibility, audibleness

to join or combine
*Despite the problems the two countries had in the past, they were able to **unite** on the issue of human rights.*
adj. united; n. union, unity

to teach to do something, often by repetition
*It took three months for her to **train** her dog to sit.*
adj. trained; n. training, trainer, trainee

memory
noun

---

fact
noun

---

cognizant
adjective

---

assemble
assembling, assembled
verb

---

expose
exposing, exposed
verb

1. the ability to recall information and experiences
2. something recollected from the past
1. *Because Sarah had a great **memory**, she was able to tell stories of her past experiences in vivid detail, even if they had happened years ago.*
2. *Nathaniel had fond **memories** of his vacation in Boston.*
v. memorize

---

something that is true
*Because Tony was very trustworthy, Sarah took everything he said as **fact**.*
adj. factual

---

to be aware of something
*He was **cognizant** that his actions could have been better carried out.*
n. cognizance

---

1. to put (something) together
2. to come together
*She will **assemble** the engine from spare parts.*
*All students will **assemble** in the cafeteria this afternoon.*
n. assembly

---

1. to reveal; to uncover
2. to make vulnerable; to put in contact with something dangerous
1. *The journalist wants to **expose** a bribery scandal in the mayor's office.*
2. *An explosion in the factory would **expose** workers to dangerous chemicals.*
n. exposure, exposé; adj. exposed

interpret
interpreting, interpreted
verb

---

demonstrate
demonstrating, demonstrated
verb

---

adjust
adjusting, adjusted
verb

---

diminish
diminishing, diminished
verb

---

acquire
acquiring, acquire
verb

to explain or understand the meaning of; to translate
*He says that he can **interpret** people's dreams.*
n. interpretation, interpreter; adj. interpretive

---

to show, to prove, or to establish (a principle, theory, etc.) with evidence
*The company said a study will **demonstrate** that their new medication is five times as effective as the medication offered by a competitor.*
n. demonstration, demonstrator; adj. demonstrable, demonstrative; adv. demonstrably, demonstratively

---

to change or alter (something) slightly in order to improve it; to modify
*You may need to **adjust** your radio antenna for better reception.*
n. adjustment; adj. adjusted

---

to become less or worse; to decline
*Her influence in the company is going to **diminish** after her successor is chosen.*
adj. diminished, diminishing

---

to obtain or receive; to attain
*During his year in Berlin he expects to **acquire** a perfect German accent.*
n. acquisition

influence
influencing, influenced
verb

---

revise
revising, revised
verb

---

absorb
absorbing, absorbed
verb

---

purchase
purchasing, purchased
verb

---

select
selecting, selected
verb

to have an effect on; to affect; to impact
*Current events **influence** her writing.*
n. influence; adj. influential, influenced

1. to reconsider
2. to improve (a piece of writing, etc.) by changing it
*Upon the discovery of Eris, astronomers decided to **revise** their definition of a planet.*
*My teacher told me that if I **revise** the essay I will get a better grade.*
n. revision, revisionism; adj. revised, revisionary, revisionist

to take in or soak up
*A sponge can **absorb** a lot of liquid.*
n. absorption; adj. absorbed, absorbing

to buy
*They are raising money to **purchase** new computers for the school.*
n. purchase, purchaser

to choose
*In the dance competition, the judges will **select** five dancers as finalists.*
n. selection, selector; adj. selective, select; adv. selectively

paradox
noun

---

pedestrian
adjective

---

invent
inventing, invented
verb

---

create
creating, created
verb

---

commemorate
commemorating, commemorated
verb

something appearing to contain a contradiction
*The fact that he never studied, but always received perfect marks on his exam, was a **paradox** to his fellow students.*
adj. paradoxical

---

1. common, not distinct
2. having to do with walking
*1. She always thought her views were eccentric, but they were actually very **pedestrian**.*
*2. There is a **pedestrian** path through the national park.*
n. pedestrian

---

to produce something new
*Alexander Graham Bell **invented** the telephone.*
n. inventor, invention

---

to make something from scratch
*He was able to **create** beautiful works of art.*
adj. created; n. creator, creation

---

to honor something; to remember something
*Each year, she **commemorates** her national championship win by watching a recording of the game.*
n. commemorator, commemoration

mention
mentioning, mentioned
verb

---

formulate
formulating, formulated
verb

---

solve
solving, solved
verb

---

intervene
intervening, intervened
verb

---

enhance
enhancing, enhanced
verb

to bring something up; to refer to something
*He tried to **mention** the power of positive thinking whenever he could.*
adj. mentioned, mentionable

---

to come up; to develop
*Before Susan took any action, she decided to **formulate** a plan.*
n. formulation, formulator

---

to come up with an answer to a problem
*After much thinking, she was able to **solve** the problem posed by her math teacher.*
adj. solved

---

to become involved in a situation; to interfere
*A fight broke out during the school dance, but the chaperones were able to **intervene** before anyone was hurt.*
n. intervention; adj. intervening

---

to make better; to improve
*Dressing neatly for a job interview will **enhance** your likelihood of getting hired.*
n. enhancement; adj. enhanced

motivate
motivating, motivated
verb

---

imply
implying, implied
verb

---

reveal
revealing, revealed
verb

---

implement
implementing, implemented
verb

---

thrive
thriving, thrived/throve
verb

to give (a person) a reason or incentive to do something; to encourage or inspire
*Our coach tries to **motivate** us to practice harder by setting goals.*
n. motive, motivation; adj. motivated

---

to suggest that something is true without saying so directly; to insinuate
*Although he didn't complain, his reaction **implied** that he was disappointed.*
n. implication; adj. implicit, implied

---

to show; to uncover
*The curtains were pulled back to **reveal** a beautiful view.*
n. revelation; adj. revealing

---

to put into effect; to enact
*We will **implement** a new grading system next semester.*
n. implement, implementation

---

to flourish; to do well; to prosper
*This plant will **thrive** in a warm, wet climate.*

strive
striving, strived/strove
verb

require
requiring, required
verb

accelerate
accelerating, accelerated
verb

respond
responding, responded
verb

reject
rejecting, rejected
verb

to try; to attempt or endeavor
*She **strove** to be a role model for female athletes.*
n. striver

---

to need or demand
*Finishing a crossword puzzle **requires** a lot of patience.*
n. requirement; adj. required

---

to gain speed; to speed up
*The gas pedal makes a car **accelerate**.*
n. acceleration

---

to answer; to reply
*It is likely that only half of the people we contact will **respond** to our survey.*
n. response, respondent, responsiveness; adj. responsive

---

to refuse to accept; to dismiss
*Very few scientists entirely **reject** this theory.*
n. reject, rejection; adj. rejected

contend
contending, contended
verb

---

consecutive
adjective

---

vital
adjective

---

amiable
adjective

---

fluent
adjective

to debate; to assert
*His opinion was very clear; he constantly **contended** that the park needed to be updated.*
n. contender, contention

---

to follow in order
*The students were asked what came next in the list of **consecutive** numbers: 1, 2, 3, 4.*
adv. consecutively; n. consecutiveness

---

1. necessary for life
2. of extreme importance
*1. Carbon dioxide is **vital** for the plant's survival.*
*2. If you want a passing grade, it is **vital** that you submit your term paper on time.*
n. vitality; adv. vitally

---

friendly; pleasant
*Even when Julie was under significant stress, she was always an **amiable** person.*
n. amiability, amiableness; adv. amiably

---

able to speak a language proficiently
*It did not take Esther long to become **fluent** in Spanish.*
n. fluency; adv. fluently

describe

describing, described
verb

---

passion
noun

---

exceed

exceeding, exceeded
verb

---

derive

deriving, derived
verb

---

invest

investing, invested
verb

to explain something
*When he went to court, he had to **describe** the event with as much detail as he could remember.*
adj. describable

a strong emotion
*She had a **passion** for working to bring about world peace.*
adj. passionate, impassioned

to go above and beyond
*His presentation **exceeded** all of their expectations.*
n. exceeder

to obtain (something) from a source
*All of the ingredients in this shampoo are **derived** from plants.*
n. derivation, derivative; adj. derived

to put money or effort into something in the hope of receiving a benefit
*She made her fortune by **investing** in the stock market.*
n. investment, investor

investigate
investigating, investigated
verb

---

decline
declining, declined
verb

---

utilize
utilizing, utilized
verb

---

seek
seeking, sought
verb

---

encounter
encountering, encountered
verb

to look closely at something in order to determine the truth; to examine
*The police are going to **investigate** his connections to organized crime.*
v. investigation, investigator; adj. investigative

---

1. to become lower or worse; to decrease or diminish
2. to choose not to do something; to refuse
1. *The price of gold is projected to **decline** next year.*
2. *If the dinner is held on a Thursday, I will have to **decline** the invitation.*
n. decline; adj. declining

---

to use
*Our system will **utilize** the most advanced technology.*
n. utilization, utility

---

to look for
*The company **seeks** applicants for a paralegal job.*
n. seeker

---

to meet; to face
*Plans for a new shopping mall always **encounter** opposition in the city council.*
n. encounter

involve
involving, involved
verb

---

anticipate
anticipating, anticipated
verb

---

modify
modifying, modified
verb

---

undergo
undergoing, underwent
verb

---

underlie
underlying, underlay
verb

to make (someone) a part of something
*I don't want to get **involved** with this; it sounds like a terrible idea.*
n. involvement; adj. involved

to expect
*Experts **anticipate** a major victory by the opposition party in this election.*
n. anticipation; adj. anticipated, anticipatory

to adapt; to change or adjust
*She wants to **modify** her car to run on solar power as well as gasoline.*
n. modification; adj. modified

to experience; to be subjected to
The website will ***undergo*** a complete remodeling.

1. to be located beneath
2. to be a cause or reason for something
1. *The layer of rock that **underlies** the earth's crust is called the mantle.*
2. *Numerous issues **underlie** the failure of the peace talks.*
adj. underlying

fiction
noun

---

abbreviate
abbreviating, abbreviated
verb

---

credible
believable, trustworthy
adjective

---

prevent
preventing, prevented
verb

---

inspire
inspiring, inspired
verb

something fake or imagined
*It wasn't until the end of his story that we learned it was **fiction**.*
adj. fictional

---

to shorten
*Because her speech was 10 minutes long, she was asked to **abbreviate** it when she presented at the next meeting.*
n. abbreviator, abbreviation

---

*It is important to get your news from a **credible** source.*
n. credibility; adv. credibly

---

to stop something from happening
*He did his best to **prevent** the accident, but he could not stop his car in time.*
adj. preventable; n. preventability

---

to motivate or influence
*The speech **inspired** her to go home and organize her apartment.*
n. inspirer, inspiration; adv. inspiringly; adj. inspirational

refer
referring, referred
verb

---

aggression
noun

---

inquire
inquiring, inquired
verb

---

undertake
undertaking, undertook
verb

---

translate
translating, translated
verb

to direct attention or action towards something
*When he asked where he could find more information, the teacher **referred** him to the textbook.*
n. referral; adj. referable

hostility; a hostile action
*When she went to the meeting, she learned of the impending **aggression** and made a plan to stop it.*
adj. aggressive

to seek out information
*When he didn't show up for school, his teacher **inquired** about his whereabouts.*
n. inquirer, inquisition

to attempt; to take on (a task or job); to tackle
*They are **undertaking** a survey of the surrounding land.*

to interpret; to express in another language
*She loves to **translate** the plays of Shakespeare into Spanish.*
n. translation, translator

terminate
terminating, terminated
verb

---

prohibit
prohibiting, prohibited
verb

---

participate
participating, participated
verb

---

discriminate
discriminating, discriminated
verb

---

comprise
comprising, comprised
verb

to end; to bring or come to a close
*If the landlord **terminates** our rental agreement, we will have to move.*
n. termination

---

to forbid or ban
*Smoking is **prohibited** in this building.*
n. prohibition; adj. prohibitive, prohibited

---

to take part in; to be involved in
*All students are required to **participate** in after-school activities.*
n. participation, participant; adj. participatory, participating

---

1. to treat differently because of prejudice
2. to detect differences, especially small or subtle ones; to differentiate or distinguish
1. *Universities cannot **discriminate** against women and minorities in their admissions practices.*
2. *Newborn babies can't **discriminate** between different colors.*
n. discrimination; adj. discriminatory, discriminating

---

to be made up of; to consist of; to incorporate
*The United States of America **comprises** 50 individual states.*

consist
consisting, consisted
verb

vary
varying, varied
verb

rely
relying, relied
verb

substitute
substituting, substituted
verb

evaluate
evaluating, evaluated
verb

to be made up (of)
*A single deck **consists** of 52 playing cards—13 of each suit.*

---

to change
*The town's population **varies** with the seasons, as many people have summer homes there.*
n. variation, variant, variance, variety; adj. various, variable, varied; adv. variously, variably

---

to be dependent (on something)
*I **rely** on the financial aid money to pay for school.*
n. reliance, reliability; adj. reliant, reliable; adv. reliably

---

to replace
*The recipe works just as well if you **substitute** oranges for lemons.*
n. substitute, substitution

---

to assess, judge, or estimate
*An engineer plans to **evaluate** the condition of the house.*
n. evaluation

acclaim
acclaiming, acclaimed
verb

---

inquire
inquiring, inquired
verb

---

diligence
noun

---

profile
noun

---

determine
determining, determined
verb

to praise; to declare or announce one's approval
*The film was highly **acclaimed** by many top critics.*
n. acclamation

---

to investigate; to question
*Because the rent was late, he was forced to **inquire** about the tenant's current employment.*
adv. inquiringly; n. inquirer, inquiry

---

significant effort put towards something
*Everyone was impressed by her **diligence**; she would not stop working until the project was completed.*
adv. diligently

---

compiled information about a person or thing
*Before she interviewed the candidate, she reviewed his **profile** in detail.*
v. profile

---

to decide based on information
*He was able to **determine** that he wanted the job after reading the job description.*
adj. determined; n. determination

engage
engaging, engaged
verb

---

resolve
resolving, resolved
verb

---

cancel
canceling, canceled
verb

---

outgrow
outgrowing, outgrew
noun

---

appreciate
appreciating, appreciated
verb

to involve in
*He wanted to **engage** her in conversation.*
adj. engaging; n. engagement

---

1. to make a decision
2. to find an answer to a problem
1. *She **resolved** to study harder for the next test.*
2. *Sandra **resolved** the problem of feeding the vegetarian guest by making a potato curry.*
n. resolver, resolution

---

to decide something will not happen; to stop from happening
*They had to **cancel** the party because of bad weather.*

---

to no longer need or be able to use (something) due to growth or development
*Mara loves this dress, but she will soon **outgrow** it.*

---

to be grateful for
*I really **appreciate** your generous help.*
n. appreciation; adj. appreciative, appreciable; adv. appreciatively, appreciably

monitor

monitoring, monitored
verb

---

construct

constructing, constructed
verb

---

establish

establishing, established
verb

---

conclude

concluding, concluded
verb

---

survive

surviving, survived
verb

to observe; to keep track of
*My parents have started to **monitor** my spending.*
n. monitor; adj. monitored

---

to build or form
*The first rule of essay writing is to **construct** a convincing argument.*
n. construction, construct; adj. constructive, constructed

---

1. to set up; to found
2. to show that something is a fact
*1. Yellowstone Park was **established** in 1872.*
*2. The prosecutor can **establish** that the defendant was there at the time of the robbery.*
n. establishment; adj. established

---

1. to finish; to end
2. to develop a judgment after studying or considering something
*1. The play **concludes** with a joyful wedding scene.*
*2. By the end of the meeting, we had **concluded** that your plan was best.*
n. conclusion; adj. conclusive, concluded, concluding; adv. conclusively

---

to last or live through an event or period of time; to endure
*Only a few books **survived** the fire in the library.*
n. survival, survivor; adj. surviving

recommend
recommending, recommended
verb

---

scrutinize
scrutinizing, scrutinized
verb

---

pollute
polluting, polluted
verb

---

simulate
simulating, simulated
verb

---

ensure
ensuring, ensured
verb

1. to advise
2. to say positive things about; to endorse
1. *The doctor will often* **recommend** *that I avoid salty foods.*
2. *My friend* **recommends** *this movie.*
n. recommendation; adj. recommended

---

to closely inspect or examine
The results were unexpected, but after **scrutinizing** *the data, we confirmed the conclusion.*
n. scrutiny

---

to contaminate or make unclean
The river has been **polluted** *by chemicals from the factory.*
n. pollution, pollutant; adj. polluted

---

to imitate; to mimic
Astronauts train in water to **simulate** *the experience of weightlessness.*
n. simulation, simulator; adj. simulated

---

to make certain; to guarantee
Snow tires should be used in the winter to **ensure** *safety on slippery roads.*

decent
adjective

---

collect
collecting, collected
verb

---

oblige
verb

---

productive
adjective

---

compete
competing, competed
verb

adequate, okay, suitable, enough
*The food was **decent,** considering the low price.*
adv. decently; n. decentness

to gather; to compile
*The team tried to **collect** as much money as possible for charity.*
n. collection

to be required to do something (often in return for a favor)
*I feel **obliged** to comply with her request because she is always helping me.*

to accomplish a lot
*He is always more **productive** when he eats breakfast.*
n. productivity, productiveness

to try to win something
*They **competed** for the grand prize in the spelling bee.*
n. competition

satisfy
satisfying, satisfied
verb

---

character
noun

---

consequence
noun

---

commence
commencing, commenced
verb

---

approach
approaching, approached
verb

to meet the requirements or expectations
*It seemed that no matter what she did, she was unable to **satisfy** her parents.*
n. satisfaction; adj. satisfactory

the traits of a person
*He has very good **character**, so I trust him to do good work.*

the result of an action
*You chose to cheat on the test, so you will have to handle the **consequences** of that decision.*
adj. consequently

to begin
*Construction of the new chemistry building will **commence** next week.*
n. commencement

to come close to
*Temperatures are expected to **approach** record highs this summer.*
n. approach; adj. approachable

consult
consulting, consulted
verb

---

distract
distracting, distracted
verb

---

enable
enabling, enabled
verb

---

assess
assessing, assessed
verb

---

persist
persisting, persisted
verb

to seek advice or information from
*You should **consult** your lawyer before signing a contract.*
n. consultation, consultancy, consultant; adj. consultative

to divert or take away someone's attention
*The music can **distract** me from my work.*
n. distraction; adj. distracting

to make able or possible
*A new computer would **enable** us to work faster.*
n. enabler

to judge the nature, quality, or degree of (something); to evaluate or appraise
*Students were asked to **assess** the accuracy of information they found on the Internet.*
n. assessment, assessor; adj. assessable, assessed

to last; to go on; to endure
*The bad weather is expected to **persist** for another week.*
n. persistence; adj. persistent; adv. persistently

devote
devoting, devoted
verb

---

cease
ceasing, ceased
verb

---

doubt
doubting, doubted
verb

---

precede
preceding, preceded
verb

---

unify
unifying, unified
verb

to commit; to dedicate
*Gandhi **devoted** his life to opposing discrimination and oppression.*
n. devotion, devotee; adj. devoted; adv. devotedly

---

to end; to conclude; to stop
*A treaty was signed last night, so the fighting can finally **cease**.*
n. cessation

---

to suspect of being untrue
*The police have begun to **doubt** her version of events.*
n. doubt; adj. doubtful; adv. doubtfully

---

to go or come before
*Twenty policemen on motorcycles **precede** the president's limousine on the way to the airport.*
n. precedent, precedence; adj. preceding

---

to bring or come together; to unite
*East and West Germany were **unified** in 1990.*
n. unification, unifier; adj. unified, unifying

illuminate
illuminating, illuminated
verb

interrupt
interrupting, interrupted
verb

consider
considering, considered
verb

promise
promising, promised
verb

protect
protecting, protected
verb

1. to brighten
2. to clarify; to enlighten
1. *The wedding planner decided to **illuminate** the reception hall with candles.*
2. *His speech on orangutans was very **illuminating**.*
adv. illuminatingly; n. illumination

---

to stop; to break
*The dinner was **interrupted** when the power went out.*
adj. interruptible, interruptive; adv. interruptedly

---

to think something over
*She **considered** his proposal carefully before making a decision.*
n. consideration

---

to commit to doing something
*He **promised** he would come to her graduation party.*
n. promise

---

to keep someone or something safe
*Her job was to **protect** the queen.*
n. protection; adv. protectively

reputation
noun

---

address
addressing, addressed
verb

---

gather
gathering, gathered
verb

---

insert
inserting, inserted
verb

---

deteriorate
deteriorating, deteriorated
verb

how someone is seen to others
*It was important to her to have a good **reputation**.*
adj. reputable

---

to discuss; to direct remarks to
*He **addressed** his concerns to the president of the company*
n. address

---

to bring together
*She went to **gather** sticks for the camp fire.*
n. gathering, gatherer

---

to put (something) into something else
*To start the program, **insert** the flash drive and follow the instructions.*
n. insertion

---

to grow worse
*The patient's condition has **deteriorated** since last night.*
n. deterioration; adj. deteriorating

correspond

corresponding, corresponded
verb

---

cooperate

cooperating, cooperated
verb

---

dominate

dominating, dominated
verb

---

facilitate

facilitating, facilitated
verb

---

retain

retaining, retained
verb

1. to be very similar to something; to match almost exactly
2. to communicate in written form
1. *The Greek letter alpha **corresponds** to the letter "A" in the Latin alphabet.*
2. *I have **corresponded** with him for several months.*
n. correspondence, correspondent; adj. corresponding

---

to work together in order to accomplish something; to collaborate
*The United States and Canada **cooperate** to fight smuggling over their shared border.*
n. cooperation; adj. cooperative; adv. cooperatively

---

to exert control over
*Our basketball team is going to **dominate** the game.*
n. domination, dominance; adj. dominant

---

to make (something) easier
*Railroads **facilitated** the settlement of the Midwestern United States.*
n. facilitator, facilitation

---

to keep or hold
*The town is said to **retain** much of its historic charm.*
n. retention, retainer; adj. retentive

complement
complementing, complemented
verb

---

compliment
complimenting, complimented
verb

---

occupy
occupying, occupied
verb

---

manipulate
manipulating, manipulated
verb

---

waive
waiving, waived
verb

to bring out the best in or supply a missing quality to; to be the ideal partner or accompaniment
*The rich flavor of the wine **complements** the steak perfectly.*
n. complement; adj. complementary

to make a positive comment about; to praise
*He **complimented** her excellent taste in music.*
n. compliment; adj. complimentary

1. to be in (a place or position); to inhabit
2. to engage, employ, or keep busy
1. *The tenants sometimes **occupy** the house for months without paying rent.*
2. *The toy can **occupy** the boy for hours.*
n. occupancy, occupant, occupier, occupation; adj. occupied

to influence or control
*He will **manipulate** his grandmother into leaving him money in her will.*
n. manipulation, manipulator; adj. manipulative, manipulated;
adv. manipulatively

to give up; to relinquish
*She wants to **waive** her right to a lawyer.*
n. waiver

conscious
adjective

---

ponder
pondering, pondered
verb

---

risk
noun

---

accommodate
accommodating, accommodated
verb

---

attend
attending, attended
verb

aware, knowing
*He was **conscious** that some would perceive his actions as wrong, but he believed he was making the right choice.*
adv. consciously; n. consciousness

---

to consider fully
*The student carefully **pondered** the question before beginning to write her essay.*

---

chance of something going badly
*When playing a full-contact sport, there is a **risk** of injury.*
v. risk; adj. risky

---

to make or provide room for
*Because he was given advance notice, he was able to **accommodate** the request.*
n. accommodation

---

to go to an event
*She really wants to **attend** the concert, so she is saving money for a ticket.*
n. attendance; adj. attender

arrange
arranging, arranged
verb

---

access
accessing, accessed
verb

---

allocate
allocating, allocated
verb

---

convince
convincing, convinced
verb

---

perceive
perceiving, perceived
verb

to set up; to put in order
*He **arranged** all of the dishware on the table before the guests arrived.*
n. arrangement; adj. arranger

---

to gain entry to
*Her badge gave her **access** to the restricted floor of the building.*
n. access; adj. accessible

---

to set aside
*He **allocated** funds for his summer vacation.*
n. allocation; adj. allocated

---

to cause (a person) to agree with a statement or opinion; to persuade
*I have to **convince** her that I am right.*
adj. convincing, convinced; adv. convincingly

---

to sense; to be aware of
*Dogs can **perceive** a greater range of sounds than humans can.*
n. perception; adj. perceived, perceptible; adv. perceptibly

attribute
attributing, attributed
verb

---

occur
occurring, occurred
verb

---

intimidate
intimidating, intimidated
verb

---

reinforce
reinforcing, reinforced
verb

---

pursue
pursuing, pursued
verb

to give credit or assign responsibility for (something) to a particular person, condition, etc.

*He **attributes** his good health to a low-fat diet and plenty of exercise.*

n. attribution; adj. attributable, attributed

---

to happen; to take place

*The burglary **occurred** late last night.*

n. occurrence

---

to challenge (a person's) confidence; to make nervous or afraid

*Her students' knowledge can **intimidate** her if she feels it is greater than hers.*

n. intimidation; adj. intimidating

---

to make stronger or more intense

*He only reads books that **reinforce** his own beliefs.*

n. reinforcement; adj. reinforced

---

to follow or chase after

*The dogs will **pursue** the fox through the field.*

n. pursuit, pursuer

concentrate
concentrating, concentrated
verb

---

ignore
ignoring, ignored
verb

---

detect
detecting, detected
verb

---

expand
expanding, expanded
verb

---

clarify
clarifying, clarified
verb

to focus; to direct one's attention to
*My teacher suggested that I **concentrate** on improving my writing.*
n. concentration

---

to pay no attention to
*Whenever my little brother annoyed me, my mother told me to **ignore** him.*
adj. ignored

---

to sense or discover something; to discern; to identify
*I could **detect** some uncertainty in her voice as she answered.*
n. detection, detective, detector; adj. detectable; adv. detectably

---

to move apart or outwards so as to take up more space; to grow
*In the 1920s, scientists discovered that the universe is **expanding**.*
n. expansion, expansionism; adj. expansive, expanding

---

to make something clearer or easier to understand; to explain
*The candidate had to **clarify** his statements about environmental policy.*
n. clarification, clarity; adj. clarified

culminate
culminating, culminated
verb

---

register
registering, registered
verb

---

reduce
reducing, reduced
verb

---

physical
adjective

---

code
noun

to finish, to reach the top
*The class **culminated** in a trip to the art museum.*
n. culmination

1. to enroll
2. to notice or be noticed
*1. She **registered** in six classes for the spring semester.*
*2. It took a moment for the seriousness of the situation to **register**.*
n. registration

to minimize; to make smaller
*To **reduce** the pain, put ice on the injury.*
n. reduction

having to do with a material trait
*I am interested in the **physical** aspect of science.*
adv. physically

1. a way of communication only a select group of people can understand
2. a set of instructions
*1. When sending defense plans, the military uses **codes** so that the messages won't be understood if they are intercepted.*
*2. Because of a mistake in the video game's **code**, it stopped working once the player exceeded 65,536 points.*
v. code, encode; n. coder

glimpse

glimpsing, glimpsed
verb

---

practice

practicing, practiced
verb

---

verbal

adjective

---

permit

permitting, permitted
verb

---

justify

justifying, justified
verb

to catch sight of
*I **glimpsed** the text message before it was deleted.*
n. glimpse, glimpser

---

to work on habitually
*When you are learning how to play an instrument, it is important to **practice** every day.*
n. practice

---

expressed in words
*The nurse required a **verbal** response before he could continue.*
adv. verbally; v. verbalize

---

to allow
*The police refused to **permit** the protest.*
n. permission, permit; adj. permitted, permissive; adv. permissively

---

to show or claim that something is right or reasonable
*She tried to **justify** her theft by claiming the money was owed to her.*
n. justification; adj. justifiable, justified; adv. justifiably

fluctuate
fluctuating, fluctuated
verb

---

deviate
deviating, deviated
verb

---

export
exporting, exported
verb

---

import
importing, imported
verb

---

regulate
regulating, regulated
verb

to vary frequently and irregularly; to vacillate
*The temperature has been **fluctuating** a lot recently, so I wasn't sure if I should wear a coat.*
n. fluctuation; adj. fluctuating

---

to differ or stray from an established standard or course; to vary or diverge
*The final version of the building will **deviate** only slightly from the original plan.*
n. deviation, deviant; adj. deviant

---

to send something out of the country, usually for sale
*Their business will **export** dairy products to Europe.*
n. exporter, export, exporting; adj. exported

---

to bring something into the country, usually for sale
*He plans to **import** wine from Europe.*
n. importer, import, importing; adj. imported

---

to control, especially by making rules; to supervise
*The government **regulates** the sale of certain medicines.*
n. regulation, regulator; adj. regulatory, regulated

provide
providing, provided
verb

qualify
qualifying, qualified
verb

succeed
succeeding, succeeded
verb

remove
removing, removed
verb

commit
committing, committed
verb

to supply
*The local bakery promised to **provide** cakes for our bake sale.*
n. provision, provider

to meet requirements; to be or become eligible
*Because they won the game, they **qualify** to play in the national tournament.*
n. qualification, qualifier; adj. qualified, qualifying

to achieve a goal
*She was able to **succeed** in getting her novel published.*
n. success; adj. successful; adv. successfully

to take (something) off or away
*You must **remove** the peel before eating a banana.*
n. removal; adj. removable

1. to promise to do something; to pledge
2. to carry out (a crime, etc.)
1. *We **committed** to working here until the end of the summer.*
2. *I never thought he could **commit** murder.*
n. commitment; adj. committed

petition
petitioning, petitioned
verb

---

hesitate
hesitating, hesitated
verb

---

technical
adjective

---

abundant
adjective

---

accomplish
accomplishing, accomplished
verb

to request
*She **petitioned** the board to change the overall grading scale.*
n. petition, petitioner

to wait; to pause
*Even when I know the answer, I often **hesitate** before giving a response.*
n. hesitation, hesitator; adv. hesitatingly

pertaining to the specialized or practical skills of science, art, or any particular profession
*The applicant knew about the field in general, but did not have any **technical** experience.*
adv. technically

more than enough
*The picnic had an **abundant** supply of hot dogs; there were many left even after everyone was full.*
n. abundance; adv. abundantly

to complete something, usually an achievement
*He was able to **accomplish** the homework assignment in half of the time he thought it would take him.*
n. accomplishment; adj. accomplished

able
adjective

---

apply
applying, applied
verb

---

confidence
adjective

---

exclude
excluding, excluded
verb

---

estimate
estimating, estimated
verb

capable, having the necessary resources
*He was surprised that he was **able** to lift the box; it was much lighter than it looked.*
n. ability

1. to use for a purpose
2. to make a request
*1. She **applied** her problem thinking skills to the project at hand.*
*2. He **applied** for financial aid.*
n. application; adj. applicable

belief in oneself
*She had a large amount of **confidence** in her basketball skills.*
adj. confident

to leave out; to omit
*The girls wanted to **exclude** the boys from the game.*
n. exclusion; adj. exclusionary, exclusive, excluded; adv. exclusively

to make an educated guess
*We **estimate** that next year's profits will be 20 percent higher.*
n. estimate, estimation; adj. estimated

legislate
legislating, legislated
verb

---

indicate
indicating, indicated
verb

---

daunt
daunting, daunted
verb

---

founder
foundering, foundered
verb

---

goad
goading, goaded
verb

to make law
*Congress **legislated** a federal minimum wage in 1938.*
n. legislation, legislator, legislature; adj. legislative; adv. legislatively

---

to show or suggest
*Your test scores **indicate** exceptional talent in math.*
n. indication, indicator; adj. indicative

---

to discourage; to intimidate
*He tried hard not to let the enormity of the situation **daunt** him.*
adj. daunting, daunted

---

to sink; to fall helplessly
*After colliding with the jagged rock, the ship started to **founder**, forcing the crew to abandon it.*
adj. foundering

---

to prod or urge
*Denise had to **goad** her sister Leigh into running the marathon with her.*

riddle
riddling, riddled
verb

---

nettle
nettling, nettled
verb

---

ply
plying, plied
verb

---

edit
editing, edited
verb

---

straightforward
adjective

to make many holes in; to permeate
*She made sure to **riddle** the box so that her hamster could breathe.*

---

to irritate
*I don't particularly like having blue hair—I just do it to **nettle** my parents.*

---

1. to use diligently; to engage
2. to join together
1. Heath needs the latest model of computer to ply his trade as a video-game tester.
*2. The weaver **plied** the fibers together to make a blanket.*

---

to change and improve a piece of writing
*Your manuscript is strong, but you need to **edit** it.*
n. editor, edition; adj. editorial; adv. editorially

---

uncomplicated, simple
*An effective speech will be **straightforward** and have a clear point.*
n. straightforwardness; adv. straightforwardly

podium
noun

---

recognize
recognizing, recognized
verb

---

delete
deleting, deleted
verb

---

display
displaying, displayed
verb

---

duplicate
duplicating, duplicated
verb

platform, lectern, booth
*The teacher always gave her lectures from the **podium**.*

---

to identify
*Even though he was wearing a wig, his sister was able to **recognize** him right away.*
adj. recognizable; adv. recognizably

---

to erase
*When her phone fell into a puddle, all of her contact information was **deleted**.*
n. deletion

---

to show
*He made a presentation to **display** all of the information he had gathered for the project.*
n. display

---

to make a copy
*She **duplicated** the records so she would have a copy if anything happened to the original.*
n. duplication

search
searching, searched
verb

---

durable
adjective

---

recur
recurring, recurred
verb

---

compare
comparing, compared
verb

---

react
reacting, reacted
verb

to look for
*When the little boy's stuffed animal went missing, his mother **searched** everywhere until she found it.*
n. search

able to last through tough conditions; enduring
*The stuffed animal was very **durable**; it stayed in good condition throughout the boy's entire childhood.*
n. durability

to happen repeatedly
*The dream **recurred** so frequently she wondered if there was a hidden meaning.*

to make note of differences and similarities (between two or more things)
*They always **compare** store prices to find the best deal.*
n. comparison; adj. comparable; adv. comparably

to act in response to; to respond
*How did your mother **react** when you told her you were getting married?*
n. reaction; adj. reactionary, reactive

convey
conveying, conveyed
verb

---

combine
combining, combined
verb

---

distribute
distributing, distributed
verb

---

promote
promoting, promoted
verb

---

consume
consuming, consumed
verb

1. to communicate or express
2. to transport
1. She tried to **convey** the seriousness of the situation, but they didn't seem to grasp it.
2. The boxes were **conveyed** to Boston by train.
n. conveyance

to put together; to blend
A spork **combines** the functions of a spoon and a fork.
n. combination; adj. combined

to give out; to divide among a group
We are going to **distribute** the money evenly among the individual group members.
n. distribution, distributor; adj. distributional

1. to support or publicize
2. to raise (someone) to a higher grade or position
1. Actors often go on television talk shows to **promote** their new movies.
2. Jay worked very hard at his job, hoping he would be **promoted**.
n. promotion, promoter

1. to buy or use up
2. to eat or drink
1. Americans **consume** 25 percent of the world's oil.
2. He **consumed** the entire pie in under ten minutes.
n. consumer, consumption; adj. consuming

distort
distorting, distorted
verb

---

eliminate
eliminating, eliminated
verb

---

injure
injuring, injured
verb

---

deplete
depleting, depleted
verb

---

transform
transforming, transformed
verb

to depict something inaccurately
*That mirror **distorts** your image so that you look taller than you are.*
n. distortion; adj. distorted

---

to get rid of; to remove or exclude
*First he became a vegetarian; now he is trying to **eliminate** milk from his diet.*
n. elimination

---

to hurt
*If you aren't careful, you can seriously **injure** yourself while skiing.*
n. injury; adj. injurious, injured; adv. injuriously

---

to use up
*Some critics worry that we are rapidly **depleting** the world's oil supply.*
n. depletion

---

to change dramatically
*The discovery of penicillin **transformed** the way doctors treat infections.*
n. transformation

formulate
formulating, formulated
verb

---

impose
imposing, imposed
verb

---

network
networking, networked
verb

---

process
processing, processed
verb

---

replace
replacing, replaced
verb

1. to create a method for doing something
2. to create something methodically
1. *The soft drink recipe was **formulated** in 1885.*
2. *The students were asked to **formulate** a conclusion based on the evidence.*
n. formulation, formulator, formula

---

to force; to establish; to obtrude
*He did not want to **impose**, but he thought his opinions should be heard.*
n. imposition; adj. imposing, imposable

---

to connect to a group of people, usually for professional purposes
*She always made sure to attend company dinners because it was a great way to **network**.*
n. network, networker

---

1. to think something over for understanding
2. to manufacture
1. *It took him a while to **process** what had happened.*
2. *The factory **processes** candy bars.*
n. process

---

to exchange for something new
*When her bicycle broke, she was forced to **replace** it.*
n. replacement

skill
noun

---

software
noun

---

store
storing, stored
verb

---

generate
generating, generated
verb

---

focus
focusing, focused
verb

something one is good at
*Public speaking is one of his many **skills**.*
adj. skilled, skillful; adv. skillfully

---

a program designed to complete a task on a computer
*The new **software** automatically corrects any spelling and punctuation errors.*

---

to hold
*She **stored** her money in a safe so that it was not accessible to others.*
n. store, storage

---

to produce; to create
*His latest movie is expected to **generate** a lot of controversy.*

---

to direct one's attention to; to concentrate
*We need to **focus** on the problem of water pollution before it is too late.*
n. focus; adj. focused

identify
identifying, identified
verb

---

persuade
persuading, persuaded
verb

---

organize
organizing, organized
verb

---

tolerate
tolerating, tolerated
verb

---

guarantee
guaranteeing, guaranteed
verb

to determine who or what a person or thing is; to recognize
*She was able to **identify** him as the man who tried to sell her a stolen watch.*
n. identity, identification; adj. identifiable, identified

---

to convince
*My parents worked hard to **persuade** me to come home over spring break.*
n. persuasion; adj. persuasive; adv. persuasively

---

1. to put in order
2. to arrange
1. *I must **organize** my desk so I can find things more easily.*
2. *They are planning to **organize** a concert to benefit local charities.*
n. organization, organizer; adj. organized

---

to allow or endure
*My boss doesn't **tolerate** lateness.*
n. tolerance; adj. tolerant, tolerable; adv. tolerantly, tolerably

---

to promise or ensure
*Can you **guarantee** that this program will work on my computer?*
n. guarantee; adj. guaranteed

contribute
contributing, contributed
verb

coincide
coinciding, coincided
verb

contradict
contradicting, contradicted
verb

recover
recovering, recovered
verb

perpetuate
perpetuating, perpetuated
verb

to give or donate
*All of the parents were asked to **contribute** twenty dollars for new soccer uniforms.*
n. contribution, contributor; adj. contributed, contributing

---

to happen at the same time
*Her visit is going to **coincide** with the annual Folk Music Festival.*
n. coincidence; adj. coincidental; adv. coincidentally

---

to oppose or challenge (a person or statement), to dispute
*He will **contradict** your version of the story.*
n. contradiction; adj. contradictory

---

to improve after experiencing a decline
*The economy **recovered** quickly after the recent recession.*
n. recovery; adj. recoverable

---

to cause (something) to last indefinitely, to sustain
*Advertisements like these **perpetuate** sexism in our society.*
n. perpetuity; adj. perpetual; adv. perpetually

session
noun

---

fail
failing, failed
verb

---

present
presenting, presented
verb

---

conduct
conducting, conducted
verb

---

mentor
mentoring, mentored
verb

a series, a time period
*The fall **session** is three months long.*
adj. sessional

---

to not succeed; to lose
*She studied night and day because she was worried she would **fail** if she didn't learn all of the material.*
n. failure; adj. failing

---

to show or demonstrate
*He **presented** the data at the national conference.*
n. presentation, presenter

---

to manage; to direct
*She **conducted** the entire operation without a hitch.*
n. conduct, conductor

---

to provide an example for; to teach; to influence
*He was happy to **mentor** the incoming freshman student.*
n. mentorship, mentor

aware
adjective

---

raise
raising, raised
verb

---

base
noun

---

preliminary
adjective

---

valuable
adjective

to know; to be cognizant
*He was **aware** of someone entering the room.*
n. awareness

---

to lift in height or status
*After she completed school, she was able to **raise** herself to new heights she had never imagined before.*
n. raise

---

the bottom layer; the starting point
*Building a successful organization requires a stable **base**.*
v. base

---

coming before or done in preparation for something
*Before starting the program, you will need to take a **preliminary** course.*
n. preliminary

---

of great worth; expensive
*The discs contained very **valuable** information.*
v. value; n. value; adj. valued

reluctant
adjective

---

subtle
adjective

---

vague
adjective

---

consistent
adjective

---

equivalent
adjective

unwilling; not eager
*He got the scholarship, but he is **reluctant** to move abroad.*
n. reluctance; adv. reluctantly

---

delicate or understated; not obvious
*Though garlic can be overpowering, in this recipe it is quite **subtle**.*
n. subtlety; adv. subtly

---

unclear; imprecise; not specific
*I don't remember exactly what she looked like, but I have a **vague** memory.*
n. vagueness; adv. vaguely

---

1. unchanging; stable
2. compatible; in line with
1. *To train your dog, you must be **consistent** about disciplining him.*
2. *The results of the blood test were **consistent** with the diagnosis.*
n. consistency; adv. consistently

---

equal
*One gallon is **equivalent** to four quarts.*
n. equivalent, equivalence, equivalency; adv. equivalently

valid
adjective

---

widespread
adjective

---

rigid
adjective

---

ultimate
adjective

---

abstract
adjective

1. acceptable as true; reasonable; convincing
2. legally binding or effective; legitimate
1. *She made a very **valid** point about the risks of this investment.*
2. *He will leave the country soon, because his visa is only **valid** until next week.*
v. validate; n. validity, validation; adj. validated; adv. validly

---

affecting or existing in a large area; extensive; general
*The storm caused **widespread** damage, with flooding in six states.*

---

hard; stiff; unyielding
*There is a **rigid** dress code at his new school that forbids jeans and sneakers.*
n. rigidity; adv. rigidly

---

1. eventual; final
2. ideal; best
1. *Her musical career started badly, but her talent and dedication ensured **ultimate** success.*
2. *This is the **ultimate** chocolate chip cookie: rich and chewy.*
n. ultimate, ultimatum; adv. ultimately

---

based on ideas or general concepts rather than physical reality or specific events
*This aspect of economics seems very **abstract**, but it has important real-life applications.*
n. abstraction, abstract; adv. abstractly

merit
noun

explore
exploring, explored
verb

flexible
adjective

achieve
achieving, achieved
verb

likewise
adverb

excellence; commendation
*She showed great **merit** when she told the truth regardless of how it would impact her.*
adj. meritorious

to examine; to search
*He loved to **explore** the woods behind his house.*
n. exploration

willing to compromise or bend
*She was usually strict when it came to travel routes, but this time she was **flexible**.*
n. flexibility

to accomplish something
*His parents were very proud of all he was able to **achieve** in school.*
n. achievement

similarly; in the same way; also
*I couldn't afford to fly home, and a train ticket was **likewise** beyond my means.*

approximately
adverb

---

hence
adverb

---

via
adverb

---

ignorant
adjective

---

extensive
adjective

close to but not precisely; nearly; about
Approximately *5 percent of Americans commute to work using public transportation.*
v. approximate; n. approximation; adj. approximate, approximated

---

as a result; therefore; consequently
*Filtering the water in the aquarium will make it cleaner, and **hence** healthier for your fish.*

---

by way of
*We flew back from Los Angeles **via** Chicago.*

---

lacking in knowledge; unaware; uneducated
*He knows a lot about most sports, but when it comes to hockey he is completely **ignorant**.*
n. ignorance, ignoramus; adv. ignorantly

---

wide-reaching; broad; substantial
*She has **extensive** experience with a variety of computer systems.*
v. extend; n. extent; adv. extensively

universal
adjective

---

positive
adjective

---

visible
adjective

---

essential
adjective

---

enormous
adjective

applying to all people or situations
*Fear of the unknown is a **universal** human trait.*
n. universality; adv. universally

---

good, not negative
*The new rules should have a **positive** effect on safety.*
adv. positively

---

able to be seen
*The fish were **visible** through the clear water.*
n. visibility; adv. visibly

---

absolutely necessary; crucial
*Good water is **essential** for making good tea.*
n. essence; adv. essentially

---

immensely large; huge
*The fossil is an **enormous** footprint that may have been made by a dinosaur.*
n. enormousness; adv. enormously

domestic
adjective

---

final
adjective

---

accurate
adjective

---

external
adjective

---

internal
adjective

1. relating to the home or housework
2. existing, originating or taking place within one's own country
1. *Women and men today are likely to share the burden of **domestic** tasks.*
2. *Voters tend to be more interested in **domestic** issues than in foreign affairs.*
n. domesticity, domestic; adv. domestically

---

last
*Tomorrow is the **final** day of classes for the fall semester.*
v. finalize; n. finality, finalization, final; adv. finally

---

perfectly correct; without errors
*She always checks her bill before paying to make sure it is **accurate**.*
n. accuracy; adv. accurately

---

on or from the outside
*Because no one at the company was able to solve the problem, an **external** consultant was hired.*
v. externalize; n. externality, externalization; adj. externalized; adv. externally

---

on or from the inside
*Technologies such as ultrasounds enable doctors to examine **internal** organs without surgery.*
v. internalize; n. internality, internalization; adj. internalized; adv. internally

obtain
obtaining, obtained
verb

verify
verifying, verified
verb

accumulate
accumulating, accumulated
verb

efficient
adjective

primary
adjective

to acquire
*After 5 years of college, he was able to **obtain** his degree in political science.*
adj. obtainable; n. obtainability, obtainer, obtainment

---

to prove true
*She was able to **verify** the information before she presented it in court.*
n. verification, verifiability, verifier; adj. verifiable

---

to collect together
*The rain water **accumulated** in the bucket he had set out to catch it.*
n. accumulation

---

streamlined
*She operated in such an **efficient** manner that she completed the task in half of the time allotted.*
n. efficiency; adv. efficiently

---

main; major; most important or significant
*Taxes were one of the **primary** reasons that the American colonies declared independence.*
n. primacy; adj. prime; adv. primarily

apprehensive
adjective

---

mature
adjective

---

annual
adjective

---

isolated
adjective

---

mental
adjective

nervous; worried that something bad will happen
*He is **apprehensive** about the interview.*
n. apprehensiveness; adv. apprehensively

---

fully grown; aged; adult
*She has become much more **mature** since she went away to college.*
v. mature; n. maturity, maturation

---

occurring once each year; yearly
*I'm taking my car to the mechanic for its **annual** inspection.*
adv. annually

---

solitary; alone
*The cabin was completely **isolated** in the middle of the forest.*
v. isolate; n. isolation, isolationism

---

relating to the mind; intellectual or psychological
*His strange behavior led doctors to suspect he was suffering from a **mental** illness.*
n. mentality; adv. mentally

ethical
adjective

---

relevant
adjective

---

prior
adjective

---

remarkable
adjective

---

beneficial
adjective

concerning or consistent with accepted moral standards; moral
*Doctors disagree about whether it is **ethical** to transplant kidneys from living donors.*
n. ethicality, ethic, ethics; adv. ethically

---

connected to what is being considered; pertinent; applicable
*The judge ruled that this information wasn't **relevant** to the case.*
n. relevance; adv. relevantly

---

preexisting; earlier
*Most students in the class have some **prior** knowledge of the subject.*

---

noteworthy; striking; extraordinary
*Since the new program began, there has been a **remarkable** increase in the number of applicants to the school.*
adv. remarkably

---

good; having a positive effect
*Vitamin A is said to be **beneficial** for the eyes.*
n. benefit; adv. beneficially

infinite
adjective

unique
adjective

secure
adjective

available
adjective

capable
adjective

endless; limitless; innumerable; so great as to be impossible to measure or count
*The universe is so immensely large that many consider it to be **infinite**.*
n. infinity; adv. infinitely

---

exceptional; special; one of a kind
*Her style is unlike anyone else's; it is **unique**.*
n. uniqueness; adv. uniquely

---

safe; assured
*Make sure to keep your valuables in a **secure** place.*
v. secure; n. security; adv. securely

---

readily obtained; possible to get
*This chair is **available** in six different colors.*
n. availability

---

able to do something; competent
*Many scientists still doubt that apes are **capable** of using complex language.*
n. capability

reflect
reflecting, reflected
verb

---

adjacent
adjective

---

desire
desiring, desired
verb

---

project
projecting, projected
verb

---

deceptive
adjective

1. to mirror; to cast back
2. to ponder
1. *His manners **reflected** his upbringing.*
2. *After the discussion, Sam **reflected** on everything Jen had to say.*
n. reflection

---

next to
*The description was **adjacent** to the photo.*
adv. adjacently

---

to want something
*She **desired** a promotion, so she worked her hardest every day.*
n. desire; adj. desired

---

1. to put one's feelings on someone else
2. to extrapolate, to predict the effects of a trend
1. *He felt responsible for the incident, so he **projected** his negative attitude onto everyone he met that day.*
2. *During the meeting, she planned to **project** the effects of the new marketing plan on the next year of sales.*
n. projection

---

misleading; giving a false impression
*The pictures were **deceptive**—the apartment was actually quite small.*
v. deceive; n. deception; adv. deceptively

intrinsic
adjective

---

contemporary
adjective

---

complex
adjective

---

crucial
adjective

---

intermediate
adjective

deeply rooted; essential; inherent
*Freedom of expression is an **intrinsic** American value.*
adv. intrinsically

---

1. existing or happening at the same time
2. existing or happening in the present; modern
*1. Her childhood was **contemporary** with the First World War.*
*2. Their house is filled with fashionable **contemporary** furniture.*
n. contemporary

---

difficult to understand; complicated
*The problem was too **complex** to be solved in a single meeting.*
n. complexity

---

extremely important; indispensable
*The helicopter is delivering **crucial** supplies to a remote hospital.*
n. crux; adv. crucially

---

situated between two stages; in the middle
*Before moving on to the advanced class, I am going to try the **intermediate** level.*

glib
adjective

---

stoic
adjective

---

potential
noun

---

overview
noun

---

phenomenon
plural: phenomena
noun

said in an insincere manner; offhand; casual
*The slimy politician managed to continue gaining supporters because he was
a **glib** speaker.*
n. glibness

indifferent to or unaffected by emotions
*While most of the mourners wept, the dead woman's husband kept up a **stoic**,
unemotional facade.*
adv. stoically

ability or promise
*Her coach thinks she has the **potential** to be a world-class athlete.*
adv. potentially

a general survey
*This book offers an **overview** of the major developments in astronomy since the
time of Galileo.*

something that exists or occurs, especially something remarkable; an
occurrence; a wonder
*The annual migration of the monarch butterflies is an incredible natural
phenomenon.*
adj. phenomenal; adv. phenomenally

foundation
noun

evidence
noun

option
noun

insight
noun

logic
noun

the base that something is built on; basis; underpinning
*Charles Darwin's theory of natural selection is the **foundation** of modern biology.*
adj. foundational

---

facts that support a theory or assertion
*Although many believed he was guilty, there wasn't enough **evidence** to prosecute him for the crime.*
adj. evident, evidential, evidenced; adv. evidently

---

a choice or possibility
*There are several different **options** for getting Internet access.*
adj. optional; adv. optionally

---

understanding or appreciation
*This book gave me greater **insight** into modern politics.*
adj. insightful; adv. insightfully

---

reason; rational thinking
*The problem has to be solved with **logic**.*
n. logician; adj. logical; adv. logically

initiative
noun

---

complicate
complicating; complicated
verb

---

fulfill
fulfilling, fulfilled
verb

---

compile
compiling, compiled
verb

---

rigorous
adjective

self-motivation; ability to start something
*Although she didn't have to, Sarah took the **initiative** to hold a bake sale for charity.*
adv. initiatively

---

to make challenging or difficult
*If he didn't get his way, he would try his best to **complicate** matters.*
n. complication; adj. complicated

---

to satisfy completely
*The meal was very **fulfilling**.*
n. fulfillment

---

to gather information
*She **compiled** the data necessary to run the reports.*
n. compilation

---

strict; demanding
*Hospitals must maintain **rigorous** standards of cleanliness.*
n. rigor; adv. rigorously

profound
adjective

---

coherent
adjective

---

passive
adjective

---

conceivable
adjective

---

sufficient
adjective

extremely intense, meaningful, or thoughtful
*He has a **profound** understanding of the plight of the poor.*
n. profundity; adv. profoundly

logical; reasonable and consistent
*To get an A on a paper, you need to have a **coherent** argument and support it with facts.*
n. coherence; adv. coherently

not actively participating; inactive
*They weren't involved in the vandalism; they were just **passive** witnesses.*
n. passivity; adv. passively

able to be thought of; imaginable
*We used every **conceivable** method to raise money for the project.*
v. conceive; adv. conceivably

enough
*The oxygen in the tank is **sufficient** for a one-hour dive.*
v. suffice; n. sufficiency; adv. sufficiently

rapid
adjective

---

adequate
adjective

---

intellectual
adjective

---

minuscule
adjective

---

intense
adjective

fast; quick
*The ambulance crew has to provide a **rapid** response in emergencies.*
n. rapidity; adv. rapidly

---

of as much quantity or quality as is needed; sufficient; enough
*The climbers left base camp with **adequate** supplies for a three-day journey.*
n. adequacy; adv. adequately

---

intelligent; relating to intelligence; academic; educated
*Because she enjoys to read, her conversations are usually very **intellectual**.*
n. intellect, intellectual; adv. intellectually

---

extremely small; minute; tiny
The water is safe to drink, but it has a **minuscule** amount of contamination.

---

extreme; severe
*People with appendicitis experience **intense** abdominal pain.*
v. intensify; n. intensity, intensification; adj. intensive, intensified; adv. intensely, intensively

ambiguous
adjective

compatible
adjective

medical
adjective

automatic
adjective

familiar
adjective

able to be interpreted in more than one way; unclear
*We had a long debate over some **ambiguous** passages in Hamlet.*
n. ambiguity, ambiguousness; adv. ambiguously

suitable for; able to work with
*His style of acting was more **compatible** with film than with television.*
n. compatibility

relating to healthcare and the science of treating diseases
*My son wants to get a **medical** degree and become a doctor or nurse.*
v. medicate; n. medicine; adv. medically

that operates or happens on its own; self-activating
*The lights are on an **automatic** timer, so they turn on every night even if no one is home.*
v. automate; n. automation; adj. automated; adv. automatically

1. acquainted; having knowledge of
2. well-known; friendly
*1. I've read many of her books, so I'm **familiar** with her theories.*
*2. It was good to see a **familiar** face after my long stay abroad.*
n. familiarity

submit
submitting, submitted
verb

---

background
noun

---

outstanding
adjective

---

reconcile
reconciling, reconciled
verb

---

normal
adjective

to yield; to give; to turn in
*Even though he wasn't in complete agreement, he was willing to **submit** to the desires of the rest of the group.*
n. submission, submitter

1. objects located behind other objects
2. experience; origin
1. *She could see her mom in the **background** of the family picture.*
2. *The agency performed a complete check on his **background**.*

excellent; superior
*Her work was so **outstanding** that she received an instant promotion.*
adv. outstandingly

to settle an argument or disagreement
*I am glad they were able to **reconcile** after all of these years.*
n. reconciliation

natural; consistent with what is expected
*Is it **normal** for a baby to walk so early?*
v. normalize; n. normality, normalization; adj. normalized; adv. normally

integral
adjective

---

comprehensive
adjective

---

objective
adjective

---

temporary
adjective

---

significant
adjective

necessary in order for something to be complete; extremely important
*You are an **integral** part of this project; we couldn't do it without you.*
adv. integrally

---

complete; thorough
*With this **comprehensive** collection of recipes, you'll never need another cookbook.*
adv. comprehensively

---

unbiased; unprejudiced
*We need an **objective** judge to tell us whose singing is better.*
n. objectivity; adv. objectively

---

lasting a short time
*This won't work forever; it's only a **temporary** solution.*
adv. temporarily

---

worthy of attention; important; remarkable
*There has been a **significant** increase in the annual number of forest fires.*
n. significance; adv. significantly

maximum
adjective

---

minimum
adjective

---

considerable
adjective

---

ethnic
adjective

---

legal
adjective

of the greatest possible amount or degree; most
*I got a ticket for driving over the **maximum** allowable speed.*
v. maximize; n. maximum, maximization; adj. maximal; adv. maximally

---

of the least possible amount or degree
*They set a **minimum** GPA of 3.5 for applicants to the honors program.*
v. minimize; n. minimum, minimization; adj. minimal; adv. minimally

---

great in amount or extent; sizable; substantial; significant
*The first European colonists in North America faced **considerable** hardships during the cold winter months.*
adv. considerably

---

cultural; united or defined by culture, tradition, or nationality
*The event was intended to promote understanding between members of different **ethnic** groups.*
n. ethnicity; adv. ethnically

---

allowed by or relating to the law; lawful
*Alcoholic beverages were banned in the United States from 1919 until 1933, when Prohibition ended and they became **legal** again.*
v. legalize; n. legalization, legality; adj. legalized; adv. legally

previous
adjective

---

distinctive
adjective

---

contrary
adjective

---

stable
adjective

---

inevitable
adjective

prior
*Do you have any **previous** experience?*
adv. previously

---

characteristic; special; unique
*Asparagus has a **distinctive** taste.*
n. distinction; adj. distinct; adv. distinctively, distinctly

---

opposite; contradictory; conflicting
*No matter what I say, you always argue the **contrary** position.*
n. contrary; adv. contrarily

---

unlikely to change or shift; secure
*It is best for children to grow up in **stable** homes.*
v. stabilize; n. stability, stabilization; adv. stably

---

impossible to prevent; unavoidable
*He was a reckless driver, and it was **inevitable** that he would eventually get into an accident.*
n. inevitability; adv. inevitably

loyal
adjective

strict
adjective

conserve
conserving, conserved
verb

prepare
preparing, prepared
verb

obvious
adjective

faithful
*No matter where he lived, he was always **loyal** to his home sports team.*
n. loyalty; adv. loyally

---

exact; precise; narrowly defined
*The teacher was known to be very **strict** because she did not tolerate anyone disobeying the rules.*
n. strictness

---

to use the least amount of; to save
*He tried his best to **conserve** water during the drought.*
n. conservation, conservationist

---

to get ready
*She **prepared** the food for the party the night before.*
n. preparation, preparer

---

easily seen or recognized; clear
*It was **obvious** that he was going to win.*
adv. obviously

mutual
adjective

---

brief
adjective

---

fundamental
adjective

---

random
adjective

---

rational
adjective

shared by or affecting both parties
*My parents made a **mutual** decision to sell the house.*
adv. mutually

---

short
*There will be a **brief** announcement before class today.*
n. brevity; adv. briefly

---

basic; essential; intrinsic
*The Supreme Court has recognized that all citizens have a **fundamental** right to privacy.*
n. fundamental; adv. fundamentally

---

without order or organization
*The seating assignments were **random**.*
n. randomness; adv. randomly

---

consistent with logic and reason; reasonable; logical
*A good judge must be **rational**, and not easily swayed by emotion.*
v. rationalize; n. rationality, rationalization, rationalist; adv. rationally

similar
adjective

---

incredible
adjective

---

predominant
adjective

---

liable
adjective

---

identical
adjective

resembling something else; alike
*Oranges and tangerines are **similar** fruits.*
n. similarity; adv. similarly

---

hard to believe; amazing; remarkable
*She has an **incredible** ability to learn new languages quickly.*
adv. incredibly

---

strongest or most prevalent; foremost; main; primary
*The cake is supposed to be chocolate mocha, but the **predominant** flavor is coffee.*
v. predominate; n. predominance; adv. predominantly

---

legally responsible
*Parents are **liable** for damage caused by their children.*
n. liability

---

exactly the same
*We hoped the other airline would be cheaper, but the ticket prices were **identical**.*
adv. identically

neutral
adjective

---

appropriate
adjective

---

global
adjective

---

mediocre
adjective

---

mandatory
adjective

belonging to neither of two opposing categories; impartial; unaffiliated

*I am liberal, but my brother is conservative, so to avoid offending either of us my mother tries to be politically **neutral**.*

v. neutralize; n. neutrality, neutralization; adj. neutralized; adv. neutrally

---

proper or suitable

*Some parents worry that these video games may not be **appropriate** for children.*

n. appropriateness; adv. appropriately

---

relating to or affecting the entire world; widespread

*After years of operating locally, we have decided to become a **global** company serving people in many countries.*

n. globe, globalization; adv. globally

---

of moderate quality or ability; unexceptional; passable

*He's an excellent guitarist, but only **mediocre** as a drummer.*

n. mediocrity

---

required; obligatory; compulsory

*Before the start of classes, new students must attend a **mandatory** orientation.*

source
noun

---

prompt
adjective

---

realistic
adjective

---

yield
yielding, yielded
verb

---

statistic
noun

origin
*They attempted to find the **source** of the leak, but were unable to tell where it was coming from.*

---

quick; speedy
*The landlord demands **prompt** payment of rent as soon as the first of the month comes around.*
n. promptness; adv. promptly

---

possible; similar to real life
*It is much easier to understand a story if the characters are **realistic**.*
adv. realistically

---

to provide; to produce
*The field **yielded** far more crops than the farmer was expecting.*
n. yield

---

information derived from numerical analysis
*The latest **statistics** show an increase in the rate of population growth.*
n. statistician; adj. statistical; adv. statistically

publication
noun

---

error
noun

---

method
noun

---

revolution
noun

---

commerce
noun

1. the act of publishing a text
2. a published book, journal, magazine, etc.
1. *He is excited about the **publication** of his first novel.*
2. *She has written articles for several different **publications**.*

---

a mistake
*This report contains an unacceptable number of **errors**.*
v. err; adj. erroneous; adv. erroneously

---

a way of doing something; a technique
*They are developing a new **method** for learning to read music.*
n. methodology; adj. methodical, methodological; adv. methodically, methodologically

---

1. a circular movement; a rotation or turn
2. a dramatic change, especially the overthrow of a government
1. *Earth completes a **revolution** around the sun every 365¼ days.*
2. *The American **Revolution** overthrew an English colonial government; the French **Revolution** unseated a native ruling class.*
v. revolve, revolutionize; n. revolutionary, revolt; adj. revolutionary

---

economic activity; trade; business
*The new policies are supposed to encourage **commerce** by helping small businesses.*
adj. commercial; adv. commercially

administration
noun

---

conflict
noun

---

partner
noun

---

innovation
noun

---

finance
noun

1. the group of people responsible for managing a company, government, etc.; management
2. the act of running an organization
1. *The proposal has to be approved by the University **administration**.*
2. *She is going to business school to get a degree in **administration**.*
v. administer, administrate n. administrator; adj. administrative;
adv. administratively

---

a state or incident of disagreement or hostility; a clash
*There is often a **conflict** between one's personal desires and the best interest of society.*
v. conflict; adj. conflicting, conflicted

---

one who shares an activity, business, etc.
*He's looking for a new tennis **partner**.*
n. partnership

---

a new way of doing something; an invention
*The VCR was a major **innovation** in the way people watched films.*
v. innovate; n. innovator; adj. innovative; adv. innovatively

---

1. the field of banking and investments
2. (in plural) a person's or company's situation with respect to money
1. *My brother is a stockbroker, and I also plan to have a career in **finance**.*
2. *My **finances** are very bad right now, and I am afraid the bank will reject my loan application.*
v. finance; n. financier, financing; adj. financial; adv. financially

behavior
noun

---

prerequisite
noun

---

phase
noun

---

wisdom
noun

---

candidate
noun

the way that a person acts; conduct
*They criticized her **behavior** during the game.*
v. behave; adj. behavioral; adv. behaviorally

---

something that must be done beforehand; a requirement or precondition
*Introductory English 101 is a **prerequisite** for the advanced creative writing course.*
adj. prerequisite

---

a stage
*Before becoming a butterfly, a caterpillar goes through a "chrysalis" **phase**.*

---

knowledge and good judgment based on experience; good sense
*The decision demonstrated his **wisdom**.*
adj. wise; adv. wisely

---

a person seeking a position, especially a person running for election to public office
*She is one of three **candidates** for governor.*
n. candidacy

tedious
adjective

---

caution
cautioning, cautioned
verb

---

collaborate
collaborating, collaborated
verb

---

agenda
noun

---

status
noun

long, boring
*The lecture was so **tedious** that many students fell asleep.*
adv. tediously; n. tediousness

---

to give warning
*He made sure to **caution** his daughter before she attempted any new activity that would put her in danger.*
adj. cautious; n. caution

---

to work together
*The finance team **collaborated** with the IT team to come up with a profitable solution.*
n. collaboration

---

a plan; an outline of events
*He was required to make an **agenda** before each class meeting.*

---

1. importance in relation to others, rank
2. condition or state
1. *People often judge the social **status** of others based on the way they dress.*
2. *Eva asked for the **status** of the report to determine how close it was to completion.*

ideology
noun

---

location
noun

---

controversy
noun

---

incentive
noun

---

outcome
noun

a strong and rigid system of belief; dogma
*Communist **ideology** was influential during the twentieth century.*
n. ideologue; adj. ideological; adv. ideologically

---

a position or site; a place
*They still haven't found a good **location** for their new restaurant.*
v. locate; adj. located

---

intense public disagreement about something; a debate
*A **controversy** arose over the school's new science curriculum.*
adj. controversial; adv. controversially

---

a reward for doing something
*To attract new members, the gym is offering **incentives** such as free yoga classes.*

---

a result
*The **outcome** of the election was a surprise to everyone.*

proficiency
noun

---

instance
noun

---

gender
noun

---

concept
noun

---

diversity
noun

ability; skill; competence
*Before studying abroad, students are expected to achieve basic **proficiency** in a foreign language.*
adj. proficient; adv. proficiently

---

an example of an action or phenomenon; an occurrence; an occasion
*It was just one more **instance** of personal success.*

---

the sex of a person
*Discrimination based on **gender** is illegal.*
adj. gendered

---

an idea, especially one that is abstract and general
*As an introduction, she explained the major **concepts** that would be covered in the class.*
v. conceptualize; n. conception, conceptualization; adj. conceptual, conceptualized; adv. conceptually

---

variety, especially in terms of culture or ethnicity
*The **diversity** of the student body has increased significantly in the past decade.*
v. diversify; n. diversification; adj. diverse, diversified; adv. diversely

leeway
noun

---

resource
noun

---

proof
noun

---

opportunity
noun

---

alternative
noun

flexibility; freedom; room for variation or to maneuver
*The camp counselors were given a lot of **leeway** in how they chose to enforce the rules.*

---

a stock of information, skill, money, etc., that can be used to make or accomplish something
*Do you have enough **resources** to carry out this project?*
adj. resourceful

---

evidence showing that a statement or fact is true; verification
*New customers are required to show **proof** that they live in the neighborhood.*

---

a chance to do something
*The recital will give him an **opportunity** to demonstrate his talent.*
adj. opportune; adv. opportunely

---

any of multiple options; another possibility
*Whole grains such as barley are exciting and healthy **alternatives** to pasta.*
adj. alternative; adv. alternatively

attitude
noun

level
adjective

repel
repelling, repelled
verb

uniform
adjective

trend
noun

feeling
*The rainy weather impacted his **attitude** in a negative way.*
adj. attitudinal

---

1. even; equal
2. rank; place on a scale
1. *The billiards table needs to be perfectly **level** to be suitable for tournament play.*
2. *The teacher offered extra study sessions for students needing help so that everyone was at the same knowledge **level**.*
n. level; v. level

---

to drive away
*The bug spray **repelled** insects from the campsite.*
n. repellant

---

consistent; the same
*It was crucial that each person completed the task in a **uniform** manner.*
n. uniformity

---

a dominant pattern or direction; a tendency
*The **trend** towards larger and larger vehicles has begun to change.*
v. trend; adj. trendy

function
noun

comment
noun

lecture
noun

emphasis
noun

analysis
noun

what something is used for; purpose or utility
*Archaeologists are uncertain about the **function** of these ancient stone tools.*
v. function; n. functionality; adj. functional, functioning; adv. functionally

---

a remark that expresses an observation or opinion
*We never had a chance to give our **comments** on the proposal.*
v. comment; n. commentary, commentator

---

a speech intended to teach something
*Are you going to Professor Smith's **lecture** on the Cold War?*
v. lecture; n. lecturer

---

special attention; stress; prominence
*The new laws put **emphasis** on protecting the environment.*
v. emphasize; adj. emphatic; adv. emphatically
plural: emphases

---

a detailed interpretation of information
*An **analysis** of the test results showed gradual improvement in math scores.*
n. analyst; v. analyze; adj. analytical, analyzed; adv. analytically
plural: analyses

hypothesis
noun

---

circumstance
noun

---

strategy
noun

---

tradition
noun

---

regime
noun

an unproven theory, especially a scientific one
*Her **hypothesis** was that the mice eating the special diet would grow twice as fast.*
v. hypothesize; adj. hypothetical; adv. hypothetically
plural: hypotheses

---

a condition or fact that affects an event or creates a situation
*The room was cold and dark, and he hadn't slept the night before; it is difficult to take a test under those **circumstances**.*
adj. circumstantial

---

a plan for how to do something; a method
*In chess, it is important to have a strong **strategy** from the beginning of the game.*
v. strategize; n. strategist; adj. strategic; adv. strategically

---

a practice or belief that has existed for a long time; a custom
*Our family has a **tradition** of eating fish for dinner on Christmas Eve.*
n. traditionalist; adj. traditional; adv. traditionally

---

a government, usually one that is oppressive and authoritarian
*Her book discusses the various groups that opposed the Nazi **regime**.*

target
noun

---

era
noun

---

authority
noun

---

generation
noun

---

hierarchy
noun

something that is aimed for; a goal
*To meet our **target**, we have to increase sales by 15 percent.*
v. target; adj. targeted

---

a long period in history that has defining characteristics
*He recommended a book about the colonial **era**.*

---

the power or right to make decisions or judgments about something
*Only Congress has the **authority** to officially declare war.*
adj. authoritative; adv. authoritatively

---

all of the people who are born within a particular period of time
*The **generation** of Americans born right after World War II are often called the "baby boomers."*

---

a fixed order of things by status or importance
*There was a strict **hierarchy** in medieval European society, with the king at the top and the peasants on the bottom.*
adj. hierarchical; adv. hierarchically

length
noun

---

period
noun

---

examine
examining, examined
verb

---

unison
noun

---

topic
noun

duration
*The **length** of the class was different on Tuesdays than on Wednesdays.*
adj. lengthy

---

amount of time
*The class **period** lasted one hour.*
adj. periodic

---

to look at thoroughly
*The scientist **examined** the specimen before making any classifications.*
n. examination

---

at the same time
*They always spoke in **unison**.*

---

a subject for study or discussion
*The **topic** of her paper is animal life in rainforests.*
adj. topical; adv. topically

principle
noun

---

boon
noun

---

fracas
noun

---

policy
noun

---

consequently
adverb

an idea that forms the foundation of a theory or of a system of morality
*The **principle** of equality is an important part of any true democracy.*
adj. principled

---

blessing; something to be thankful for
*Dirk realized that his new coworker's computer skills would be a real **boon** to the company.*

---

noisy dispute
*When the players discovered that the other team was cheating, a violent **fracas** ensued.*

---

a procedure for dealing with or approach to a public issue
*The administration is developing a new **policy** on immigration.*

---

as a result; for this reason; therefore; accordingly
*Regular exercise leads to better health and, **consequently**, to a longer life.*
n. consequence; adj. consequent

subsequently
adverb

---

definitely
adverb

---

nevertheless
adverb

---

initially
adverb

---

furthermore
adverb

following this; later; afterwards; thereafter
He retired from his banking job at age 65 and **subsequently** *became involved in charity work.*
adj. subsequent

---

certainly; assuredly
It is **definitely** *going to be sunny tomorrow.*
adj. definite, definitive; adv. definitively

---

in spite of that; nonetheless
Educational opportunities for women were limited in the nineteenth century; **nevertheless**, *women contributed to that era's scientific accomplishments.*

---

in the beginning; to begin with; at the start
The cost of owning a car turned out to be much higher than we **initially** *expected.*
adj. initial

---

in addition; additionally; moreover
She likes the biology program at that university, and **furthermore**, *they offered her a scholarship.*

overall
adverb

---

eventually
adverb

---

recently
adverb

---

chiefly
adverb

---

thereby
adverb

on the whole; in general
*Sally's pizza has a great crust, but I think Pepe's pizza is better **overall**.*

in the end; ultimately
*He can only say a few words now, but **eventually** he will be able to speak fluently.*
n. eventuality; adj. eventual

in the not too distant past; not long ago
*I have always been very healthy, but I **recently** started feeling sick.*
adj. recent

mostly; mainly; primarily
*The book focuses **chiefly** on social history.*
adj. chief

in this way; as a result of this
*She came in second in the race and **thereby** earned a spot on the national team.*

disrupt
disrupting, disrupted
verb

---

experiment
noun

---

goal
noun

---

progress
progressing, progressed
verb

---

majority
noun

to interrupt; to destroy
*Her sleep was **disrupted** by the dog barking outside.*
n. disruption, disruptor

---

trial; test
*He performed many **experiments** in his science class.*
v. experiment; n. experimenter

---

the desired result
*She always set realistic **goals** for herself.*

---

making forward motion
*As long as he **progressed** towards his goals each day, he was confident he would reach them.*
n. progression

---

the largest part of a whole; more than half
*The **majority** of Americans prefer coffee to tea.*

minority
noun

---

talent
noun

---

data
noun

---

media
noun

---

narrative
noun

1. a small part of a whole; less than half
2. a member of a group that accounts for less than half of a population
1. *Atheists are a **minority** in the United States.*
2. *The company is recruiting **minorities** for positions on its board of directors.*

---

skill or ability
*She has an amazing **talent** for music.*
adj. talented

---

information
*The report is based on **data** collected over 25 years.*
singular: datum

---

news and entertainment outlets such as newspapers, television, radio, and film
*The politician was happy with the way he had been depicted in the **media**.*
singular: medium

---

a story; an account of connected events
*The Odyssey is a long **narrative** in the form of a poem.*
v. narrate n. narration; adj. narrative; adv. narratively

tactic
noun

---

symbol
noun

---

duration
noun

---

expert
noun

---

labor
noun

a plan or technique for achieving a goal; a strategy
*The new **tactic** introduced by our coach helped us win the game.*
n. tactician; adj. tactical; adv. tactically

---

an image, etc., that represents something else; a sign
*The raven in the poem is often interpreted as a **symbol** of death.*
v. symbolize; n. symbolism; adj. symbolic; adv. symbolically

---

the length of time that something lasts
*Please remain seated for the **duration** of the flight.*

---

a person who has special knowledge or experience in a particular field
*The museum called in an **expert** to determine if the painting was a forgery.*
n. expertise; adj. expert; adv. expertly

---

work, especially physical work
*Without a ride-on mower, mowing your lawn can be exhausting **labor**.*
v. labor; adj. laborious; adv. laboriously

bias
noun

---

decade
noun

---

genre
noun

---

perspective
noun

---

text
noun

an attitude that is unfairly positive or negative about a particular group, person, or thing in comparison to others; prejudice
*The company is accused of **bias** against the elderly in its hiring practices.*
adj. biased

a period of ten years
*The Great Depression of the 1930s lasted an entire **decade**.*

a style or category, especially a type of literature, etc.
*She prefers books in the **genre** of science fiction.*

a point of view
*I'd like to hear your **perspective** on this issue.*

a piece of writing
*The class will discuss **texts** by six major twentieth-century thinkers.*
adj. textual

supervise
supervising, supervised
verb

---

anxious
adjective

---

respond
responding, responded
verb

---

dedicate
dedicating, dedicated
verb

---

income
noun

to oversee or manage
Even though it was not her responsibility, she always took on the task of **supervising** *operations.*
adj. supervised

---

stressed; uneasy
Because he did not feel prepared for the test, he became very **anxious***.*
n. anxiousness; adv. anxiously

---

to answer
She always made sure to **respond** *to emails as soon as she read them.*
n. response

---

to devote
He **dedicated** *his life to world peace.*
n. dedication

---

money that is paid to a person or company; salary; earnings
If she gets promoted, her **income** *will increase substantially.*

assumption
noun

---

priority
noun

---

summary
noun

---

structure
noun

---

theory
noun

a belief that is not based on proof
*Historians must be careful not to make **assumptions** about the past based on today's values.*
v. assume; adj. assumed

something considered to be of the highest importance
*We will eventually paint the house, but right now our **priority** is to finish the roof.*
v. prioritize; n. prioritization

a short description of the content of a longer piece of writing, film, etc.
*We were asked to write a one-page **summary** of the book.*
v. summarize; n. summarization; adj. summarized

1. the way in which the parts of something are put together; organization
2. a building or construction
*1. The **structure** of a typical essay involves an introduction at the beginning and a conclusion at the end.*
*2. The ruins include a large, low **structure** that might have been used to store grain.*
v. structure; adj. structural, structured; adv. structurally

a system of ideas that is meant to explain a complex phenomenon; a belief, thesis, or hypothesis
*Scientists are developing new **theories** about the nature of the universe.*
v. theorize; n. theorist; adj. theoretical; adv. theoretically

revenue
noun

---

appearance
noun

---

climate
noun

---

research
noun

---

impact
noun

income; money that is earned
*The store has had much higher **revenues** this year.*

---

the way something looks
*It is a beautiful old house, but the broken windows ruin its **appearance**.*
v. appear; adj. apparent; adv. apparently

---

weather conditions over a long period of time; the environment
*Scientists are studying the forces causing changes in the **climate**.*
adj. climatic

---

intensive study of a particular topic
*He is doing **research** on local history.*
v. research; n. researcher

---

an impression; an effect
*The film had a great **impact** on me; I was really moved.*
v. impact; adj. impacted

challenge
noun

---

individual
noun

---

region
noun

---

sequence
noun

---

exception
noun

1. a difficult task or undertaking
2. a questioning of authority
1. *The marathon is a **challenge** even for experienced runners.*
2. *Impressionist paintings were seen as a **challenge** to traditional artistic standards.*
v. challenge; n. challenger; adj. challenging, challenged

---

a single person
*Identical twins often complain that people tend to treat them as a pair, rather than as **individuals**.*
n. individuality, individualism, individualist; adj. individual, individualistic, individualized; adv. individually

---

a large area that is considered to have unifying characteristics
*The southwestern **region** of the United States is known for its desert climate.*
adj. regional; adv. regionally

---

order
*The numbers in the code have to be entered in the right **sequence**.*
v. sequence; adj. sequential, sequenced; adv. sequentially

---

something that is not like others of its type; an anomaly
*Most mammals give birth to live young; the platypus, which lays eggs, is an **exception**.*
adj. exceptional; adv. exceptionally

spur of the moment

---

elephant in the room

---

with child

---

grandfathered in

---

push the envelope

spontaneously or impulsively; without prior planning
*They were supposed to stay home this weekend, but on the **spur of the moment** they decided to go camping instead.*

---

something that is very apparent that no one is talking about
*We need to stop procrastinating and discuss the **elephant in the room**.*

---

pregnant
*She didn't drink at the party because she is **with child**.*

---

something that is prohibited by new rules, but is allowed to continue because it existed before the rules came into play
*Bars are no longer allowed on this street, but Joe's Pub is **grandfathered in**.*

---

to do something new and different that goes beyond what was previously thought to be possible; to innovate
*His new website really **pushes the envelope** of what the Internet can be used for.*

abide by the rules

carry on doing something

test the waters

pan out

account for something

to accept and follow (a law, ruling, etc.); to comply with
*Both companies claim the right to sell the product, but they will **abide by** the judge's decision.*

---

to continue
*The book was so interesting that he **carried on** reading it after the end of study hall.*
*They will **carry on** with the dance lessons until they master the tango.*

---

to check the likelihood of success before proceeding
*Before announcing their new initiative, the politicians **tested the waters** by conducting polls to assess the likely public response.*

---

to yield good results; to turn out well
*She has had several job interviews, but nothing has **panned out** yet.*
[from *to pan for gold*: to attempt to extract gold from a river]

---

to explain; to provide an explanation for
*The police asked him to **account for** the missing money.*
*The full moon **accounts for** the exceptionally high tide today.*

give it away

---

follow suit

---

grow out of something

---

back up data

---

know the ropes

to reveal (information that was supposed to be kept secret)
*The party was supposed to be a surprise, but my little sister **gave it away**.*

---

to do the same; to follow the example set by someone else
*She decided to skip the tournament and the rest of the team **followed suit**.*
[a reference to card games in which all players must play a card of the same suit as the one led by the first player]

---

1. to become too large for (something); to outgrow
2. to develop on the basis of (something)
1. *She gives her son's clothes to charity when he **grows out of** them.*
2. *This book **grew out of** a series of lectures I gave last year.*

---

to make an electronic copy (of a computer file, etc.) as security in case the original is damaged or deleted
*The power outage wasn't a problem because we had already **backed up** the files on the computer.*

---

to understand how things are done in a particular place
*To succeed in a new job, ask someone who really **knows the ropes** to train you.*
Hence, to **show someone the ropes** means "to show someone how things are done."
[a reference to sailing ships with complicated ropes and riggings]

back someone **into a corner**

---

have second thoughts

---

look after a child

---

look forward to an event

---

look into something

to put (someone or oneself) into a position where there is no way out and no room to maneuver
*His political opponents tried to **back** him **into a corner**, so that any position he took would cause him to lose support.*
*She has **backed** herself **into a corner** by setting the standards so high that no one—including her—can meet them.*

---

to reconsider
*After I saw the reading list, I **had second thoughts** about taking the class.*

---

to take care of
*She **looks after** her little brother after school every day.*

---

to anticipate (something) with pleasure
*I'm **looking forward to** the concert next week.*

---

to investigate; to seek information about
*We are **looking into** buying a camper for our summer trip.*

cut a person some slack

---

first-rate

---

off base

---

touch base with

---

keep one's options open

to give someone a break, to be understanding
*My boss knew that I was going through a hard time, so when I missed the deadline he **cut** me **some slack**.*

---

of high quality
*The accommodations in that hotel were **first-rate**.*

---

missing the point, not understanding
*I don't think she watched the news program properly; the conclusions she drew were way **off base**.*

---

check in with
*Even if my manager is having a busy week, he always makes time to **touch base with** me and catch up on my project work.*

---

to avoid doing anything that might rule out a future course of action
*She will probably matriculate to State University, but she's **keeping** her **options open** until she has gotten a response from all of the schools she applied to.*

bring the facts **home** to someone

---

bring new information **to light**

---

see the light

---

look up

---

look something **up**

to make (the reality of something) clear
*This book finally **brought** the complexity of the issue **home** to me.*

to reveal; to uncover
*Their study **brought to light** some long-forgotten manuscripts.*

to finally realize something after serious consideration
*I thought he would never agree with me, but eventually he **saw the light**.*

to show signs of improvement
*She had more tests done and the doctors say her health is **looking up**.*

to seek information about (something) in a reference work
*I **looked up** the words I didn't know in a dictionary.*

look up to someone

---

give someone **free rein**

---

rein someone **in**

---

give her story **the benefit of the doubt**

---

hold one's **own**

to have respect and admiration for someone
*He had always **looked up to** his uncle, who was a teacher.*

---

to put few restrictions on the behavior of (someone)
*The new teacher **gives** the students **free rein** to study whatever they want.*
[A rein is the strap used to control a horse while riding.]

---

to control (someone's) behavior closely
*Whenever she began to stray from the task our supervisor **reined** her **in**.*

---

to assume that (a person or statement) is truthful until proven otherwise
*His alibi is suspicious, but let's **give** him **the benefit of the doubt** until we know more.*

---

to perform reasonably well in a challenging situation
*The other runners in the race are much more experienced, but she is **holding** her **own** and will probably finish right in the middle.*

hold one's **tongue**

---

bring something **to mind**

---

set the record straight

---

use up a resource

---

size up the competition

to stay silent; to refrain from speaking
*He was upset and wanted to say something, but he **held** his **tongue**.*

---

to be reminiscent of (something); to remind
*This dish **brings to mind** a meal I once had in Paris.*

---

to correct a false story; to provide accurate information
*The media initially reported that the escaped animal was a tiger, but zoo officials **set the record straight** by announcing that it was a kangaroo.*

---

to consume (something) completely
*I couldn't brush my teeth this morning because my brother had **used up** the toothpaste.*

---

to evaluate or assess
*The dogs growled and walked in a circle, **sizing** each other **up**.*

back down

---

back off

---

seeing things

---

second nature

---

have one's **hands tied**

to give up, to walk away from
*He always had to prove how tough he was; he never **backed down** from a fight.*

leave alone, let it be
*She is having a rough time; you should **back off**.*

seeing something that is not really there
*I could have sworn I saw him walk into his room 10 minutes ago, but he isn't home. I must have been **seeing things**.*

something that comes naturally
*After she gave birth, taking care of her son was **second nature** to her.*

to be restricted; to be prevented from doing something
*I wish I could give you more information, but my **hands are tied**.*

lower the bar

---

flare up

---

ask after someone

---

hold sway

---

go through with something

to reduce standards so that it is easier to succeed
When no one qualified under the original criteria, the admissions committee **lowered the bar.**

---

to erupt or break out; to recur
My doctor had said the rash on my knee was cured, but it **flared up** *again.*

---

to inquire about the well-being of (someone)
He heard your mother was in the hospital and called to **ask after** *her.*

---

to dominate; to have great influence
The Dutch **held sway** *in New York until 1664, when the English took control.*

---

to perform (an action) as planned; to carry out
We **went through with** *our plan to have a picnic in spite of the rain.*

end up

---

lay claim to property

---

cross one's **mind**

---

hold on to

---

hold out

to come eventually to a particular situation or place
*It **ended up** costing much more than we expected.*
*After walking for hours, they **ended up** in the same place they started.*

---

to assert that one has the right to something; to claim ownership of
*My sister always **laid claim** to the top bunk bed, so I was stuck on the bottom.*

---

to occur to one
*I'm so accustomed to flying that the possibility of driving home never **crossed my mind**.*

---

to keep or retain
*He considered selling his motorcycle, but he decided to **hold on to** it.*

---

to resist or endure in a challenging situation
*Her doctor advised her to give up meat, and she **held out** for six months before giving in to temptation.*

leave no stone unturned

---

cross paths

---

run into someone

---

have one's **work cut out for**

---

get one's **act together**

to look everywhere; to attempt everything
*We **left no stone unturned** in our search for the city's best hot dog.*

to meet by chance
*They **crossed paths** in Italy when they both happened to be vacationing there.*
*She **crossed paths** with my sister in college.*

to meet (someone) by chance
*I hadn't seen him in months, but I **ran into** him at the supermarket last week.*

to have a lot of work to do in order to accomplish something
*If she wants to finish this drawing before the art fair, she **has** her **work cut out for** her.*

to prepare oneself to accomplish something; to get organized
*We need to **get** our **act together** if we're going to finish this by Friday.*

on occasion

on the dot

back to the drawing board

third degree

drop by

sometimes
On occasion, *I like to shop at the mall a couple of hours away because it has great sales.*

---

at that exact time
We are meeting at 6:00 p.m. *on the dot.*

---

to start from the beginning
Our permit was not approved, so we need to go *back to the drawing board.*

---

intense interrogation
When I arrived home late, my father gave me the *third degree.*

---

to make a short, usually unannounced, visit
He *dropped by* *for a few minutes last night.*

drop in on someone

---

have one's **hands full**

---

go wrong

---

err on the side of caution

---

rest on one's **laurels**

to make a short, usually unannounced, visit to (a person)
*On the way home we **dropped in on** my grandmother to see how she was doing.*

---

to be very busy; to have a lot to do
*She has **had** her **hands full** lately, so she probably won't be able to help you.*

---

to cause a failure; to go amiss
*The experiment failed, but scientists still aren't sure what **went wrong**.*

---

to act in a reserved manner to prevent issue
*No one knows what level of pollutants is safe for fish, so it seems best to **err on the side of** conservation by stopping all pollution in the river.*

---

to be satisfied with one's past accomplishments rather than attempting anything new
*Since his highly praised first novel came out, he has been **resting on** his **laurels** and hasn't written anything new.*
[a reference to the ancient Greek tradition of crowning a person with a wreath of laurels, or bay leaves, to honor a great accomplishment]

take one's **time**

---

tighten one's **belt**

---

touch on a subject

---

see eye to eye

---

have a say

to proceed slowly; to avoid rushing
*I'm **taking** my **time** on this paper, since it isn't due until the end of the semester.*

---

to take extreme measures in order to economize; to cut back
*Our funding has been cut, so we are going to have to **tighten** our **belts** and reduce the budget.*
[a reference to losing weight from eating less, which might cause someone to need a smaller belt]

---

to address (a topic) briefly
*The course will mainly cover the works of Jean-Jacques Rousseau, but it will also **touch on** some of his contemporaries, such as Voltaire and Diderot.*

---

to have similar opinions; to understand each other
*They have almost nothing in common, but when it comes to baseball they **see eye to eye**.*

---

to have a degree of influence or power
*It is important for children to **have a say** in decisions about their activities.*
*In a democracy, citizens **have a voice** in their government.*

cherry-pick

---

do someone **good**

---

narrow down a list

---

draw a blank

---

do one's **best**

to take only the most desirable items available from among a selection
*She sells the most cars because she **cherry-picks** the most promising customers, leaving the rest of us with the reluctant ones.*

to have a beneficial effect on (someone)
*He has seemed very stressed out lately; a vacation will **do** him **good**.*

to reduce the number of options in (a selection)
*They started with a pool of twenty applicants, but they **narrowed** it **down** to three finalists.*

to be unable to remember or respond
*I studied thoroughly for the test, but when I saw the first question. I just **drew a blank**.*

to try as hard as possible
*She didn't get a perfect score, but she **did** her **best**, and that is what really matters.*

pull the plug

pull someone's leg

six feet under

mom-and-pop

throw down the gauntlet

to end something
*The principal **pulled the plug** on the old school lunch program, opting for a new, healthier alternative.*

to joke or trick someone
*I really thought he had failed his class, but he was just **pulling** my **leg**.*

deceased, dead
*I went to call her, but Martha told me she is **six feet under**.*
[referring to the depth at which people are buried.]

small, family run business
*My favorite restaurant is a **mom-and-pop** place down the road.*

to issue a challenge
*The American colonists **threw down the gauntlet** to England in 1776 with the Declaration of Independence.*
[A gauntlet is a type of armored glove, which would traditionally be thrown down by a medieval knight in a challenge to an opponent. To accept the challenge, the opponent would pick up the glove; hence, to **take up the gauntlet** means "to accept a challenge."]

throw in the towel

---

throw someone **to the wolves**

---

fill someone **in**

---

fill in for someone

---

take someone's **place**

to accept defeat; to surrender
*We struggled for many years with our business, but we finally **threw in the
towel** after realizing we needed to make major renovations.*

---

to leave (someone) to face criticism or challenges alone; to abandon
(someone)
*He claimed not to know anything about the scandal, and **threw** his assistant **to
the wolves**.*

---

to inform (someone) fully; to give (someone) the details
*Lisa missed the meeting during which that was discussed, so someone will
have to **fill** her **in**.*

---

to replace or substitute for
*I usually work on Mondays and Fridays, but I'm **filling in for** Mark today.*

---

to replace or substitute for (someone)
*The star of the play got sick, so the understudy **took** her **place**.*

come to grips with a challenging concept

---

stay out of a dispute

---

wear thin

---

speak out on a controversial issue

---

think up

to become capable of dealing with or understanding
*Many companies still haven't **come to grips with** the new regulations.*

---

to avoid getting involved in
*The United States **stayed out of** the First World War until April of 1917.*

---

to become less effective due to overuse
*You claim to have forgotten your homework at least once a week, so that excuse is **wearing thin**.*

---

to express one's opinions openly
*It was nice to hear a politician **speak out** about the problems facing farmers today.*

---

to invent; to make up
*Our math teacher is always **thinking up** new ways to make sure we do our homework.*

take advantage of someone or something

carry out orders

meet someone **halfway**

meet one's **match**

keep a low profile

1. to exploit (someone)
2. to utilize or avail oneself of (something)
1. *They had no interest in really being his friends; they were only **taking advantage of** him.*
2. *She is trying to **take advantage of** the many cultural experiences the city has to offer.*

---

to obey; to put into action
*He **carried out** your instructions perfectly; everything is the way you wanted it.*

---

to compromise with (someone)
*We made several good offers, but she stubbornly stuck to her original price and refused to **meet** us **halfway**.*

---

to find one's equal
*He is a great chess player, but at yesterday's tournament he finally **met** his **match**.*

---

to avoid getting attention or publicity
*Like many celebrities, she started **keeping a low profile** after she had children.*

piece of cake

---

slap on the wrist

---

taste of your own medicine

---

a picture is worth a thousand words

---

get a message **across**

something that is easy
*She never needed to study math; each test was a **piece of cake** for her.*

minor punishment
*Even when a celebrity commits a major crime, he often walks away with just a **slap on the wrist**.*

treatment similar to how you have been treating people
*One day, someone will treat you poorly and you will get a **taste of your own medicine**.*

you can learn more from a single picture than from many words
*She had always tried to explain the scenery around her until she learned that **a picture is worth a thousand words**.*

to express
*The president's latest speech really **got across** his concern about the need for more educational funding.*

get away with a crime

think on one's **feet**

wash one's **hands of**

settle for

cast doubt on something

to manage to escape the consequences of (an action)
*I can't believe he **got away with** cheating on that quiz.*

---

to react quickly and effectively without prior preparation
*She had to **think on** her **feet** when she was unexpectedly asked to lead the discussion.*

---

to claim to no longer be responsible for or involved with (something); to dissociate oneself from
*He **washed** his **hands of** the group after it participated in a controversial protest last year.*

---

to accept less than desired or expected
*She had dreamed of becoming president, but she **settled for** being mayor of a small town.*

---

to make (something) appear doubtful or dubious
*The photos from the party **cast doubt on** his version of events.*

make a point of doing something

---

make do

---

make sure

---

make sense

---

keep an eye on something

to make a deliberate effort to do something
*I **make a point of** calling my grandmother once a week.*

---

to manage without something important; to get by
*During the Second World War cooks often **made do** without rationed ingredients like chocolate and sugar.*

---

to be certain; to confirm
*Before leaving the house, he **made sure** he had his keys.*

---

to be reasonable or logical
*Her theory **makes sense**.*

---

to watch; to monitor
*Could you please **keep an eye on** the cake in the oven and make sure it doesn't burn?*

get over a setback

---

take someone's **word for it**

---

take a break

---

draw the line

---

think better of

to recover from; to bounce back from
*She is finally **getting over** her cold.*
*The team needs to **get over** today's loss and start preparing for the next game.*

to believe someone without additional evidence
*He says that he didn't take the money, and I'm **taking** his **word for it**.*

to take a rest; to stop an activity temporarily
*She painted for hours at a time without **taking a break**.*

to set a limit about how far one is willing to go
*I'll help you out one more time, but that is where I **draw the line**.*

to decide against (doing something) after thinking about it more; to reconsider
*She had planned to take part in the prank, but she **thought better of** it and stayed home.*

at the drop of a hat

---

an arm and a leg

---

bend over backward

---

cross your fingers

---

think something **over**

in a moment
*If she ever called, he would come to her side **at the drop of a hat**.*

---

a large amount of money
*A gallon of milk used to be so inexpensive; now it costs **an arm and a leg**.*

---

to be overly accommodating, to do a large amount for someone
*Whenever she needed anything, he would **bend over backwards** for her.*

---

a gesture made for good luck
*I am going in for a big job interview today, so **cross your fingers** for me!*
*Sheila's getting surgery done tomorrow; **keep your fingers crossed**!*

---

to consider (something) carefully
*I probably won't accept the job offer, but I am still **thinking** it **over**.*

think twice

get rid of something

get the best of someone

get to the bottom of a mystery

get underway

to consider carefully before making a decision

*If I were you, I would **think twice** about buying a used car over the Internet. When he was invited to give a speech at his old high school, he didn't **think twice** before agreeing.*

---

to discard or eliminate

*We **got rid of** all the food in the refrigerator that was past its due date.*

---

to defeat or outwit

*She tried to stay awake for the fireworks at midnight, but her fatigue **got the best of** her and she fell asleep before 11:00.*

---

to uncover the truth about

*We reported the strange sounds coming from the house next door and the police promised to **get to the bottom of** it.*

---

to begin; to start

*The annual Autumn Festival **gets underway** next week.*

mince words

jump on the bandwagon

make good on a promise

make off with

stand for something

to avoid directly saying something which might upset or offend
Tell me what you really thought of my performance and don't **mince words**.

---

to take up an activity or idea that is suddenly very popular
The price of the stock rose quickly as investors **jumped on the bandwagon** *and bought shares.*

---

to follow through on
The company **made good on** *its pledge to donate new computers to the school.*

---

to take or steal (something)
He was caught after the party trying to **make off with** *two silver vases.*

---

1. to support or advocate (a belief or principle)
2. to be an abbreviation of
1. *The memorial should express the ideals she* **stood for** *all her life: freedom and equality.*
2. *FBI* **stands for** *Federal Bureau of Investigation.*

stand up for someone

stand out

wind down

wind up somewhere

keep at a task

to defend; to advocate for
*She always **stood up for** her little brother when other children teased him.*

---

to be conspicuous; to attract attention
*The white flowers **stand out** against the dark background of the painting.*

---

1. to slow down, to draw to a close
2. to relax (said of a person)
*1. The wedding season hits its peak in June and starts to **wind down** in September.*
*2. After three days of tough hiking, we spent a day **winding down** at the beach.*

---

to find oneself in a place or situation; to arrive or end up
*I was as surprised as anyone when I **wound up** working in the television industry.*

---

to continue to do; to persist or persevere with
*He had trouble at first, but he **kept at** it and is now one of the best gymnasts in the state.*

hit the books

---

hit the hay

---

hit the nail on the head

---

eighth wonder

---

keep information **from** someone

to study
*I didn't study at all over spring break; now it is time to **hit the books**.*

---

to go to sleep
*I didn't sleep well yesterday, so I am going to **hit the hay** early tonight.*

---

to understand something precisely
*You just **hit the nail on the head**; I knew you would understand.*

---

something remarkable
*I don't understand how their science experiment ever worked; it is the **eighth wonder** of the world.*
[in reference to the seven wonders of the world]

---

to hide (something) from someone; to keep (something) secret from someone
*Romeo and Juliet **kept** their marriage **from** their families.*

keep from doing something

---

keep up with someone or something

---

lend a hand

---

jump to conclusions

---

sit around

to stop oneself from doing something; to refrain from or avoid
*When she saw his new haircut, she could hardly **keep from** laughing.*

---

1. to travel at the same speed as; to stay abreast of
2. to stay informed about
1. *She couldn't **keep up with** the other cyclists on the hilly part of the course.*
2. *I try to **keep up with** the latest advances in computer science.*

---

to help
*Local charities **lent a hand** to the effort to rebuild after the earthquake.*
*Could you please **give** me **a hand** with this heavy box?*

---

to form an opinion about something quickly without examining all of the facts
*A good doctor looks at all of a patient's symptoms carefully before making a diagnosis rather than just **jumping to conclusions**.*

---

to lounge or be idle; to hang around
*He used to exercise a lot, but now he just **sits around** playing video games.*

sit through

---

sit tight

---

get on with an activity

---

take a piece of information **into account**

---

show up

to stay to the end of (an event or performance)
*I wanted to leave the play at intermission, but my parents made me **sit through** all three hours of it.*

---

to wait patiently
*Could you just **sit tight** for a little bit longer? I'm almost ready to leave.*

---

to continue
*We need to stop wasting time and **get on with** studying for the exam.*

---

to consider; to give attention to
*The theory was flawed because it didn't **take into account** the importance of environmental factors.*

---

to arrive
*She didn't **show up** at work until after 11:00 a.m.*

show someone **up**

---

split hairs

---

go without saying

---

take something **in stride**

---

wipe something **out**

to embarrass or outperform (someone)
He **showed up** the team captain by making the most goals in last night's game.

to make small, unimportant distinctions
They still haven't agreed on the final wording of the contract, but they are just **splitting hairs** now; all of the important issues have been decided.

to be obvious or self-evident
It **goes without saying** that you should wear respectful clothes to a job interview.

to deal with (something difficult) in a calm way, so that it does not cause disruptions
The players **took** the insults of the opposing team **in stride** and focused on winning the game.

to destroy (something) completely
Three years of drought **wiped out** the region's strawberry crop.

off the hook

off the record

on the fence

throw someone **under the bus**

save one's **breath**

to get away with something, to suffer no punishment
*The cop let him **off the hook** with a warning.*

something that is not written down
*Everything she told me, she told me **off the record**.*

not able to decide
*I really want to go to Miami for spring break, but I am **on the fence** because it is very expensive.*

to leave someone else to take the blame
*When he got caught with the stolen money, he claimed he didn't know anything about it and instead **threw** his partner in crime **under the bus**.*

to refrain from saying something that is useless or unnecessary
*She won't stop smoking no matter what you say, so **save** your **breath**.*

save face

fill out a form

bide one's **time**

keep her **on** her **toes**

keep track of

to preserve one's dignity or honor; to avoid embarrassment
*Larry **saved face** by resigning from his job before he could be fired.*

---

to complete (a form)
*He has **filled out** all of his college applications.*

---

to wait patiently
*She's living with her parents for a while, **biding** her **time** until she finds the right apartment.*

---

to force (someone) to stay alert
*Our teacher **keeps** us **on** our **toes** by asking questions throughout his lectures.*

---

to keep a record of; to stay informed about
*She **kept track of** her expenses so that she could be reimbursed.*

slip someone's **mind**

---

pave the way

---

take it easy

---

ring a bell

---

put something **to rest**

to be forgotten by someone
*I was supposed to buy milk on the way home, but it completely **slipped my mind**.*

---

to make future accomplishments possible; to prepare the way
*The achievements of pioneering female scientists like Marie Curie **paved the way** for later generations of women in science.*
[*Way* is an old-fashioned word for road; *paving* a road makes it easier and faster to travel on.]

---

to relax; to be idle
*Last summer I worked 40 hours a week, but this year I am **taking it easy**.*

---

to bring back a memory; to sound familiar
*I don't recognize his face, but his voice **rings a bell**.*

---

to put a stop to; to end; to quell
*If you are afraid of flying, the new technology in these planes should **put** your fears **to rest**.*

pin down the details

---

field questions

---

count as

---

count on

---

keep something **at bay**

to define firmly; to figure out
*The wedding is supposed to be this summer, but they haven't **pinned down** the date yet.*

---

to answer questions from a group of people
*After her speech, she **fielded questions** from the audience.*

---

to be considered; to qualify as
*Astronomy 101 **counts as** a science course for the school's distribution requirement.*

---

to rely on; to depend on
*We need to be home early because Mom is **counting on** us to help her with dinner.*

---

to make (something) stay away; to ward off
*I've been **keeping** the flu **at bay** by resting and drinking lots of orange juice.*
*The moat around the castle was designed to **keep** invaders **at bay**.*

start from scratch

---

to the nines

---

let on

---

icing on the cake

---

figure out

start from the beginning
*When he changed his mind about the topic of his world history paper, he wasn't able to use anything he had done so far; he had to **start from scratch**.*

---

to perfection
*When she went to the wedding, she was dressed **to the nines**.*

---

to admit or acknowledge
*I think he knows more than he is willing to **let on**.*

---

an added benefit
*She loves the job offer and was extremely excited to take it; the extra vacation time was just **icing on the cake**.*

---

to determine or conclude
*The mechanic **figured out** that the problems were being caused by a leak in my car's fuel line.*

cut back on something

---

cut off

---

cut to the chase

---

come around

---

come down to

to use or do less of (something)
*His doctor told him that he should **cut back on** eating sugar.*

---

1. to interrupt
2. to stop or discontinue
*1. She rudely **cut** him **off** in the middle of his story.*
*2. The storm **cut off** the city's supply of electricity.*

---

to get directly to the point
*She started describing all of the different features, but we were in a hurry, so we asked her to **cut to the chase**.*

---

to agree to something eventually
*My father didn't like the idea of me going to college so far away from home, but I'm sure he'll **come around**.*

---

to have as an essential point; to be dependent upon
*There are all sorts of fad diets around, but healthy weight loss **comes down to** two factors: eating well and exercising regularly.*

come along

---

bear fruit

---

take its **toll**

---

put off an activity

---

pass up an opportunity

1. to accompany
2. to progress
1. *He invited a friend to **come along**.*
2. *There were a lot of construction problems at first, but the new house is finally **coming along**.*

---

to produce results; to be successful
*After twenty years of research, our effort to cure the disease is finally **bearing fruit**.*

---

to have a negative effect
*The drought **took** its **toll** on the crops, and the harvest was much smaller than usual.*
*She looks exhausted. All of those late nights of studying are finally **taking** their **toll**.*

---

to postpone
*Our teacher **put** the test **off** until next week.*

---

to decline; to fail to take advantage of
*He **passed up** a scholarship at a prestigious university because the school didn't have a good soccer team.*

put one's **finger on** a piece of information

---

fall apart at the seams

---

fall short

---

fall into place

---

fall out with someone

to identify; to pinpoint
*There must be something missing, but I can't **put** my **finger on** what it is.*

---

doing very poorly, extremely unwell
*We are worried about her; ever since she was laid off, she has been **falling apart at the seams**.*

---

to fail to meet expectations
*Our profits for last year **fell short**.*

---

to turn out as hoped for
*We were afraid that we would never finish planning our wedding, but every-thing seems to be **falling into place**.*

---

to have a serious disagreement
*They **fell out with** each other years ago over who would run the family business.*
Also as a noun: to have a **falling-out** with someone.

turn a blind eye to a problem

---

cry wolf

---

gut feeling

---

actions speak louder than words
phrase

---

take note of something

to ignore; to overlook
*The superintendent accused local schools of **turning a blind eye to** plagiarism and cheating.*

---

to claim something is happening when it isn't
*He said he was about to fall over the edge, but he was just **crying wolf**.*

---

the feeling of your intuition
*I had a **gut feeling** something was wrong, so I gave her a call.*

---

what you do is more important than what you say
*He is always saying how much he cares, but then he is never around. He doesn't realize that his **actions speak louder than** his **words**.*

---

to notice; to observe
*He didn't immediately **take note of** her new haircut.*

muddle through

bring someone **up to date**

put something **on hold**

rule out a possibility

play down an achievement

to find a way in spite of difficulty or disorganization; to manage
*I didn't know anything about how to direct a play, but I **muddled through**.*

---

to give (someone) the latest information
*Since you have been absent, talk to me after class and I will **bring** you **up to date**.*

---

to stop (something) temporarily; to suspend
*We are **putting** the renovation **on hold** until next summer.*

---

to exclude (something) as a possible option or explanation
*We haven't decided where to spend our honeymoon yet, but we have **ruled out** going on a cruise.*
*The doctor told her that tests had **ruled out** cancer as the cause of her symptoms.*

---

to minimize the importance of
*The other students were impressed by his famous mother, but he always **played down** his glamorous background.*
[The opposite is to **play up:** "to exaggerate."]

play it safe

---

play with fire

---

keep something **in mind**

---

bargain for

---

deal with a situation

to avoid taking risks
*They **played it safe** and allowed two hours for the drive to the airport.*

---

to do something dangerous or risky
*We warned the diplomat that she was **playing with fire** by getting involved in local politics.*

---

to remember and account for (something)
*While writing your essay, **keep in mind** that you will get a higher grade if it has a clear argument.*

---

to expect or be prepared for
*The vacationers got more rain than they had **bargained for** when monsoon season hit a few weeks early.*

---

to handle or control
*They are finding new ways of **dealing with** the rising cost of college tuition.*

take over something

---

run out of something

---

take on someone or something

---

beat around the bush

---

put down roots

to take control of
*He is difficult to work with because he usually tries to **take over** the most interesting projects.*

---

to use up (a supply of something)
*I couldn't make cookies because I **ran out of** sugar.*

---

1. to hire (an employee)
2. to confront; to fight against
1. *They decided to **take** her **on** as a research assistant.*
2. *The environmental group is **taking on** a big corporation it accuses of polluting the lake.*

---

to avoid talking directly about something
*The community meeting was frustrating because the mayor kept **beating around the bush** instead of addressing the important issues facing our community.*

---

to settle down; to establish a permanent residence
*After years of traveling, he is finally **putting down roots** by buying a house in his hometown.*

great minds think alike
phrase

---

the ball is in your **court**
phrase

---

third time's a charm
phrase

---

tie the knot

---

put up with something unpleasant

intelligent people think the same way
*After I told her my plan, she told me that it was exactly what she had been planning; **great minds think alike**.*

---

it is your decision
*Now that you have all the information, **the ball is in** your **court**.*

---

you are likely to succeed on the third try
*I missed the bus both mornings so far this week; hopefully, the **third time's a charm**.*

---

to get married
*They have been dating for ten years and are ready to **tie the knot**.*

---

to endure or tolerate
*Rather than disciplining students who are late for class, he **puts up with** their behavior.*

take part

---

take sides

---

talk someone **into** doing something

---

put the cart before the horse

---

make up one's **mind**

to participate
*Fifty nations **took part** in the conference at which the Charter of the United Nations was drafted in 1945.*

---

to align oneself with one of the sides in a dispute
*Parents should avoid **taking sides** when their children argue.*

---

to convince (someone) to do something
*She didn't want to join the team, but they **talked** her **into** it.*

---

to do things in the wrong order
*Critics say that buying furniture for the new library before the architect has been chosen is **putting the cart before the horse**.*

---

to decide; to make a decision
*He got into three different colleges, so now he is trying to **make up** his **mind** about which one to attend.*

pay the price for something

---

take a stab at doing something

---

part with something

---

take something **with a grain of salt**

---

have mud on one's **face**

to bear the consequences of a mistake or misdeed
*The school principal made the whole class **pay the price** for graffiti made by one student.*

---

to try; to make an attempt
*I've never baked a pie before, but I'm **taking a stab at** it this weekend.*
*They asked her to **take a stab at** creating a web page.*

---

to give (something) up
*Even when he went to college, he refused to **part with** his teddy bear.*

---

to be skeptical about (something)
*Since she has strong views on this subject, you should **take** her report **with a grain of salt**.*

---

to be embarrassed
*When the newspaper published an article about his company's financial problems, the executive **had mud on** his **face**.*

wear many hats

---

worth one's **salt**

---

off guard

---

on an even keel

---

above board

to fill many roles
*As a mother, teacher, volunteer, and musician, she **wears many hats** in her everyday life.*

---

competent at one's profession
*Any coach **worth** his **salt** would have taught you how to stretch your muscles after practice.*

---

unprepared
*She did well for most of the interview, but she was caught **off guard** by the last question.*

---

steady and balanced; moving calmly forward
*The local economy went through some difficult times when the factory closed, but it has been **on an even keel** for many years.*
Also **even-keeled**: *He has an **even-keeled** personality.*
[A **keel** is a structure on the bottom of a boat that keeps it stable.]

---

conducted lawfully and openly; legitimate; honest
*The deal sounded suspicious, but my lawyer assured me that it was completely **above board**.*

best of both worlds

---

make a long story short

---

wine and dine

---

judge a book by its cover

---

blue-collar

get the positive aspects of two things at once
*I just got a new job offer to write a book from home, so I will be doing what I love and spending time with my family; it is truly the **best of both worlds**.*

---

to shorten a story to get to the point
*To **make a long story short**, she isn't coming to the meeting.*

---

to impress someone, usually with a fancy meal and drinks
*Whenever new clients came to town, he did his best to **wine and dine** them.*

---

to judge by appearance instead of merit
*She didn't look like a nice person, but when I talked to her I was pleasantly surprised. It just goes to show you should never **judge a book by its cover**.*

---

involving or denoting physical labor
*During the summer he does **blue-collar** jobs like construction work and house painting.*

white-collar

---

run-of-the-mill

---

on the tip of one's **tongue**

---

beside the point

---

to the point

denoting administrative or clerical work that does not involve physical labor
*The Internet boom has created a lot of office jobs for **white-collar** workers.*

---

unexceptional; ordinary
*Despite all of the attention she has gotten in the press, I think she is really just a **run-of-the-mill** portrait painter.*

---

on the verge of being remembered
*I can't quite recall his name, but it's **on the tip of** my **tongue**.*

---

irrelevant; unimportant
*The real issue in the renovation is that we need more space; the color of the carpet is **beside the point**.*

---

directly related to the topic at hand; relevant
*The testimony of the star witness in the case was concise and **to the point**.*

at a loss for words

---

neither here nor there

---

down to earth

---

down and out

---

in check

unable to think of anything to say; speechless
*When they told her father they were getting married, he was **at a loss for words**.*

---

unimportant or irrelevant
*We accept anyone who can play chess; your age is **neither here nor there**.*

---

reasonable and practical; realistic
*She seems remarkably **down to earth** for the daughter of a wealthy celebrity.*

---

very poor; destitute
*A decade ago, he was a **down-and-out** alcoholic, but today he owns his own business and has been sober for eight years.*

---

under control
*Now that our rent is higher, we will have to keep our spending **in check**.*

beside oneself

---

full-fledged

---

no-win situation

---

win-win situation

---

in charge of

extremely agitated or upset; distraught
*He came home three hours late and his mother was **beside herself** with worry.*

---

complete; mature; fully developed
*Her hobby of baking cookies has become a **full-fledged** business, with stores all over the city.*

---

having no possibility of a positive outcome
*It was a **no-win** situation: we either had to pay the fine or pay a lawyer to fight it.*

---

denoting a situation in which both parties benefit
*He will get professional experience and you will get a web page at a discount: it's a **win-win** arrangement.*

---

responsible for; in control of
*You will be **in charge of** refreshments for our next meeting.*

when it rains, it pours
phrase

---

when pigs fly
phrase

---

your guess is as good as mine
phrase

---

break a leg

---

on the right track

when one good/bad thing happens, many good/bad things happen
*I woke up late, spilled coffee down the front of my shirt and hit traffic on the way to work; **when it rains, it pours**.*

---

unlikely to happen
*She will be on time for class **when pigs fly**.*

I'm not any more certain than you are
*I think he said we should be there at 4:00 p.m., but **your guess is as good as mine**.*

---

have good luck
***Break a leg** in your performance tonight!*

---

following a course that is likely to be successful
*I don't know the answer yet, but I think I am **on the right track**.*

on the wrong track

---

on the fence

---

on the horizon

---

red-handed

---

is short for

following a course that is likely to fail
She hasn't been making progress with her research, and seems to be **on the wrong track**.

---

undecided; unable to make up one's mind
He is still **on the fence** *about which candidate to vote for.*

---

coming up in the future
We aren't very busy at the moment, but we have some major projects **on the horizon**.

---

in the act of committing a crime
They caught the thief **red-handed**, *with the stolen jewelry in her pockets.*

---

used as an abbreviation or shortened form of
Did you know that the word "info" **is short for** *"information"?*
Also **for short**: Theodore is called Ted **for short**.

wrapped up in something

---

up in the air

---

in short supply

---

low-key

---

feeling up to something

preoccupied with; completely absorbed in
*He was so **wrapped up in** the baseball game on television that he didn't hear me walk in.*

---

unresolved; not yet settled
*We are going to go on vacation this summer, but we haven't decided where yet; our plans are still **up in the air**.*

---

scarce; insufficiently available; running out
*We have plenty of food left, but water is **in short supply**.*

---

relaxed; laid-back; restrained
*We are having a party, but it won't be anything big, just a **low-key** gathering of friends.*

---

ready for or able to do something
*It is a very steep mountain; are you sure you're **feeling up to** going on the hike?*

in the pipeline

---

on the same page

---

in touch with someone

---

at a premium

---

in the wings

on the way; being developed
*She published two books last year and she already has another one **in the pipeline**.*

---

in complete agreement
*They had some arguments about the renovation in the beginning, but now they are **on the same page**.*

---

in contact with; in communication with
*We used to be close friends, but I haven't been **in touch with** him for several years now.*
*I really hope that I will keep **in touch with** my college roommates after we graduate.*

---

particularly valuable; especially in demand
*In today's job market, computer skills are **at a premium**.*

---

ready to act or be used at any time
*Newspaper columnists often keep one idea **in the wings** in case of writer's block.*
*There were many people waiting **in the wings** to take over when she retired.*
[a reference to the *wings* of a theater, where actors wait to go on stage]

let the cat out of the bag

once in a blue moon

a penny for your thoughts
phrase

cut corners

in the works

to tell a secret
*The party was supposed to be a surprise, but his best friend accidentally **let the cat out of the bag**.*

---

rarely
*She only calls if she needs something, which only happens **once in a blue moon**.*

---

a way to ask someone what they are thinking
*You have been awfully quiet; **a penny for your thoughts**?*

---

take shortcuts
*In order to save money, he often **cuts corners**, which will likely cost him more money in the long run.*

---

being planned or produced; in process
*A sequel to that movie is **in the works**.*

in line with something

---

at the mercy of

---

on top of a task

---

time-honored

---

on the table

in accordance with; consistent with
*The themes of her most recent novel are **in line with** her previous work.*

---

completely under the control of; powerless against; totally dependent upon
*Medieval peasants were often **at the mercy of** their local lord.*
*The small ship was **at the mercy of** the storm.*

---

doing everything necessary to accomplish (something); in control of
*I offered to help with the decorations for the dance, but the committee chair said he was **on top of** it.*

---

traditional; long-standing
*Serving turkey with cranberry sauce at Thanksgiving is a **time-honored** custom in the United States.*

---

up for discussion; possible as an option
*We haven't made a final decision yet, so all of the proposals are still **on the table**.*

of few words

---

out of the question

---

worse for wear

---

thin-skinned

---

light years ahead

not talkative; reticent
*My grandmother is a woman **of few words**, but when she says something, it is usually very insightful.*

---

impossible; inconceivable; not worth considering
*Because of the recent snowstorm, driving over the mountain was **out of the question**.*

---

showing signs of age or use
*This sofa was beautiful when it was new, but it is getting a bit **worse for wear**.*

---

extremely sensitive; easily upset
*When students are too **thin-skinned**, it can be difficult to give them feedback on their work.*
The opposite is **thick-skinned**.

---

far ahead; far more advanced
*Their science laboratories are **light years ahead** of the facilities at our university.*

out of hand

---

grass-roots

---

fine tuning

---

easy as pie

---

one in a million

unmanageable; out of control
*The absenteeism in this class is getting **out of hand**.*

---

based on the efforts of ordinary people
*Our new city councilwoman didn't get a lot of support from powerful politicians, but she had a strong **grass-roots** campaign.*

---

minor adjustments needed to perfect something
*The car is running now, but we have to do some **fine tuning** to make it ready to drive on the road.*
Also as a verb: *We need to **fine-tune** our performance.*

---

very simple
*Since he had studied so hard, he thought the exam was **easy as pie**.*

---

unique; unusual
*The company knew they'd found **one in a million** when they hired her for the job.*

IDIOM LIST 16

wet behind the ears

---

green

---

foregone conclusion

---

odds and ends

---

level playing field

new; untested
*He doesn't know yet how his company's e-mail system works, because he's only been there one day and is still **wet behind the ears**.*

---

inexperienced; new
*Her first interview with the mayor went too long, because she was **green** and didn't know which questions to ask.*

---

an obvious outcome; a result which can be predicted in advance
*Because of the home team's superior defense, it was a **foregone conclusion** that they would win.*

---

an assortment of random things
*His desk was covered with **odds and ends**, so it was impossible to find anything.*

---

fairness; equality
*Public schools are intended to create a **level playing field** in education.*

mixed emotions

---

the powers that be

---

light at the end of the tunnel

---

white elephant

---

lame duck

positive and negative feelings felt at the same time
*She has **mixed emotions** about moving away; she's excited about the new house, but worried about going to a new school.*

---

the people who have authority
*No changes can be made without approval from **the powers that be**.*

---

hope that a time of difficulty will end
*Xavier struggled to get out of debt for years, but he finally sees the **light at the end of the tunnel**.*

---

a possession that is useless or unwanted, and difficult to get rid of
*The painting is valuable, but no one wants a picture of a slaughterhouse, so it's really a **white elephant**.*

---

a person who is currently in a position of authority, but whose successor has already been chosen
*When a sitting U.S. president loses the election for a second term in November, he becomes a **lame duck** until the new president is inaugurated the following January.*

second wind

---

last minute

---

last resort

---

last straw

---

white lie

a new burst of energy or strength to continue a difficult effort
*In the last week before the play opened, the actors got their **second wind** and rehearsed long hours to ensure that it was a success.*
[originally used to describe the sudden ability to breathe more easily that some people feel after exercising for a long time]

the latest possible time
*She always leaves her homework until the **last minute**.*
Also as an adjective: ***last-minute** Christmas shopping.*

the final option remaining when everything else has failed
*Doctors consider surgery for weight loss the **last resort** and recommend it only for people who are not helped by diet, exercise, or medication.*

the last of a series of problems or annoyances, which causes someone to finally give up
*We have put up with a leaky roof, dripping faucet, and heating problems in this apartment, but the roaches were the **last straw**; we are going to move out tomorrow.*

a lie considered to be harmless, often told out of politeness
*I told him he looked nice, but it was a **white lie**; his tie was really ugly.*

salt of the earth

---

yellow journalism

---

the lesser of two evils

---

red tape

---

small talk

a person who is decent, honest, kind, and unpretentious
*Her parents are very nice people, the **salt of the earth**.*
Often used as an adjective: ***salt-of-the-earth*** *people*.

---

journalism that is sensationalist and biased
*That newspaper will print anything to sell papers—it's all gossip and **yellow journalism**.*

---

an option which is bad, but still better than the alternative
*I wasn't impressed with either of the candidates, but I voted for **the lesser of two evils**.*

---

excessive regulations and bureaucracy
*We had to deal with a lot of **red tape** to get the proper visa to travel here.*
[from the red-colored tape or ribbon that was once used to tie together bundles of legal documents]

---

polite conversation on unimportant topics; chat
*He made **small talk** with all of the guests at the party.*

tip of the iceberg

---

no time to lose

---

double-edged sword

---

sticking point

---

zero tolerance

a small but easily recognized part of a much larger problem or issue
*The corruption scandals reported in the news are only the **tip of the iceberg**.*
[a reference to the fact that most of an iceberg is hidden underneath the water—only the tip is visible]

---

no extra time, meaning it is necessary to do something right away
*There is **no time to lose**, so let's get to work.*

---

something that has the potential both to help and to hurt
*Her talent is a **double-edged sword**: it brings her success, but it has also limited her options.*

---

a controversial issue that is an obstacle to making an agreement
*They are close to signing a contract, but the number of vacation days is still a **sticking point**.*

---

a policy of punishing even minor offenses
*The school has instituted a policy of **zero tolerance** for dress code violations; last week, a student got detention for forgetting to wear a tie.*
Also as an adjective: *a **zero-tolerance** approach to law enforcement.*

mint condition

---

upper hand

---

bad blood

---

game plan

---

cutting edge

---

in excellent condition, as if new
*These antique toys are very valuable because they are still in **mint condition**.*
Also as an adjective: *a **mint-condition** car*.
[in reference to *mint*, a place where coins are made]

the better position in a situation; the advantage
*When the other team's best player was suspended, we gained the **upper hand**.*

hostility due to past events; ill will; antagonism; hatred
*There has been **bad blood** between them ever since the lawsuit ten years ago.*

a strategy
*What is your **game plan** for increasing profits?*

the forefront of progress within a field
*This scientist is doing projects on the **cutting edge** of physics research.*
Also used as an adjective: ***cutting-edge** technology*.

Achilles' heel

a clean slate

gray area

face value

about face

the one weak spot of an otherwise strong person
*Though I am generally good in English, his first question found my **Achilles' heel**: my ignorance of spelling rules.*
[in reference to the character *Achilles* in Greek mythology, who could be injured only on his heel]

---

a fresh start, with any previous mistakes forgiven or forgotten
*She moved to a new school, where she could start over with **a clean slate**.*

---

an issue about which there is no clear answer, or where conventional standards don't seem to apply
*A lot of Internet businesses operate in a **gray area**, and no one is sure what laws should apply to them.*

---

1. the value printed on a ticket, note of currency, etc.
2. the apparent or superficial meaning of something
*1. We paid more than **face value** for the concert tickets.*
*2. If you take his last speech at **face value**, it sounds like he is planning radical changes.*

---

a complete reversal; a U-turn
*After ten years of supporting the same party, she did an **about face** and started voting for the opposition.*

what it takes

---

vicious cycle/circle

---

eleventh hour

---

bitter pill

---

uncharted waters

the qualities required to accomplish something
*Your daughter has **what it takes** to be a professional musician.*

---

a cycle of negative effects that build off of one another, resulting in a worsening situation; a downward spiral
*Some overweight children get caught in a **vicious cycle**: they don't excel at athletics because of their weight, so they get less exercise, which in turn makes them even more overweight.*
*Because the shop didn't have enough inventory, customers didn't come to it; because there weren't enough customers, the shop couldn't afford more inventory. It was a **vicious circle**.*

---

the last possible moment
*They waited until the **eleventh hour** to make plans for their trip, so they had trouble getting a hotel room.*
Also as an adjective: *an **eleventh-hour** effort to conclude the talks.*

---

an unpleasant fact that is difficult to accept
*The knee injury that ended his tennis career was a **bitter pill**, but he became a successful coach.*

---

a new or unfamiliar situation
*Advances in biotechnology are taking scientists into **uncharted waters** requiring new ethical guidelines.*

rule of thumb

---

hard feelings

---

true colors

---

bells and whistles

---

salad days

a general or approximate guideline
*When cooking rice, a good **rule of thumb** is to use two parts water to one part rice.*

---

negative feelings of resentment or bitterness
*They are no longer in business together, but they are still friends and there are no **hard feelings** about the end of their partnership.*

---

a person's real or authentic character
*She seems very calm and polite, but her angry outburst yesterday revealed her **true colors**.*

---

attractive but unnecessary extra features
*For a little bit more money, you can get the deluxe version of the car with all the **bells and whistles**.*

---

the days of one's youth, regarded either as a time of inexperience or as a peak or heyday
*We recalled the rash decisions of our **salad days**.*

labor of love

---

olive branch

---

the big picture

---

ill-gotten gains

---

quantum leap

a project undertaken purely out of pleasure or interest
*He paints portraits for money, but his still-life paintings are a **labor of love**.*

---

a gesture of peace
*After a hard-fought campaign, the winning politician offered her opponents an **olive branch** by inviting them to join her cabinet.*

---

the broad perspective on an issue; the overview
*The proposal should focus on **the big picture**; we don't want to get bogged down in the details.*

---

profits or benefits acquired unfairly or illegally
*Robin Hood is both a thief and a hero, because he shares his **ill-gotten gains** with the poor.*

---

a sudden and significant improvement or advance
*In the past decade there has been a **quantum leap** in our scientific understanding of human genetics.*
[from physics, where a *quantum leap* is the abrupt shift of an electron within an atom from one energy state to another]

state of the art

---

recipe for disaster

---

hollow victory

Pyrrhic victory

---

ivory tower

the latest, most up-to-date technology
*His new stereo is the **state of the art** in audio equipment.*
Also as an adjective: ***state-of-the-art*** *technology.*

---

a plan or set of circumstances that is doomed to produce terrible results
*Assigning the two of them to work on a project together is a **recipe for disaster**.*

---

a victory that accomplishes or signifies nothing
*She won the race, but since all of the best competitors had dropped out, it was a **hollow victory**.*

---

a victory that comes at too high a cost, leaving the winner worse off
*Nuclear deterrence is based on the fact that to win a nuclear war would be a **Pyrrhic victory**.*

---

a place that is insulated from the concerns of the real world
*To really understand social issues, he needs to get out of the **ivory tower** of university life.*

change of pace

---

bottom line

---

across the board

---

at odds with

---

off the cuff

a change from what is usual or ordinary
She usually drinks coffee every morning, but today she's having tea for a ***change of pace***.

---

the most important consideration or conclusion; the main point
*We talked about a lot of techniques for time management, but the **bottom line** is that we just need to get more done.*
[from the use of *the bottom line* in accounting, where it refers to the final total of a balance sheet]

---

for all; in every category
*The new budget makes cutbacks in government services **across the board**, from highways to education.*

---

in contradiction to; in disagreement or conflicting with
*His account of events is **at odds with** the story published in the newspaper.*

---

without any preparation
*Everyone was impressed when she gave a fantastic speech **off the cuff**.*

now and then

---

hand in hand

---

in the dark

---

down the road

---

ahead of time

occasionally
*He doesn't exercise much, but he does go biking **now and then**.*

---

1. while holding hands
2. in close association; jointly
1. *Couples walked down the street **hand in hand**.*
2. *Low unemployment often goes **hand in hand** with inflation.*

---

without important information; uninformed
*She was upset that they had kept her **in the dark** about their plan to sell the house.*

---

in the future
*This may seem like a risky investment now, but I am confident that it will have benefits **down the road**.*

---

in advance; beforehand
*He practiced an acceptance speech **ahead of time** just in case he won the prize.*

at stake

---

in the wake of

---

through thick and thin

---

to speak of

---

without a doubt

at risk; in question
*The national championship is **at stake** in this game.*

---

as a consequence of; in the aftermath of
***In the wake of** the recent earthquake we decided to redesign the building for stability.*

---

through good times and bad times; in all circumstances
*Married couples vow to support each other **through thick and thin**.*

---

worth mentioning
*She doesn't have any savings **to speak of**; she spends all of her money on entertainment.*

---

certainly; absolutely; unquestionably
*It was **without a doubt** the worst book I have ever read.*

on top of

---

out of the blue

---

as far as someone **knows**

---

on one's **mind**

---

behind closed doors

in addition to; besides
On top of *all of his other accomplishments, he is now captain of the hockey team.*

---

without any warning; unexpectedly; out of nowhere
*I hadn't seen her in months, but she called me **out of the blue** last week and invited me to dinner.*

---

based on the information (a person) has; to the best of (a person's) knowledge
*He isn't here yet, but **as far as** I **know** he is still planning to come.*

---

in one's thoughts; preoccupying one
*I have a lot **on** my **mind** right now.*

---

in secret; out of public view
*The government eventually signed the treaty, but we may never know what bargains were made **behind closed doors** to make it happen.*

on behalf of someone

---

be that as it may

---

under the table

---

firsthand

---

on and off/off and on

as a representative of someone; in the interest of someone
*He wrote a letter **on behalf of** his mother, asking the company to give her a refund.*

---

nevertheless
*Some say that printed books are becoming obsolete; **be that as it may**, publishing remains a dynamic and prosperous business.*

---

without proper permission or disclosure; illegally
*She was getting paid **under the table** to avoid taxes.*

---

personally; directly; in person
*I had heard that the Grand Canyon was impressive, but I didn't appreciate its enormity until I saw it **firsthand**.*

---

with interruptions; intermittently
*It rained **on and off** all night, but never for very long.*
*I didn't get much sleep last night, it was **off and on** throughout the night.*

in a nutshell

---

down the line

---

to a fault

---

word of mouth

---

behind someone's **back**

in a short summary; very briefly
*This book covers the major points of the topic **in a nutshell**.*

---

in the future; eventually
*This may seem like a good policy now, but it could cause major problems **down the line**.*

---

excessively; so much that it causes problems
*She is careful **to a fault**; it takes her forever to finish anything.*

---

through informal conversation
*They didn't have enough money to advertise in the newspaper, but they got a lot of publicity by **word of mouth**.*
Also as an adjective: ***word-of-mouth*** advertising.

---

when someone is not around
*It is unfair to criticize him **behind** his **back**, when he can't defend himself.*

behind the scenes

---

all of a sudden

---

beyond a/the shadow of a doubt

---

in the balance

---

in over one's **head**

out of public view

*The agreement between the two leaders seemed spontaneous, but a lot of negotiations were conducted **behind the scenes** to make it happen.*

[a reference to theaters, where preparations take place behind the scenery, out of sight of the audience]

---

without any warning; instantly

*We were walking in the park when, **all of a sudden**, the lights went out.*

---

without any doubt at all; for certain

*We now know, **beyond a shadow of a doubt**, that the Vikings reached North America centuries before Columbus.*

---

at stake; at risk

*Applying to college is very stressful; sometimes it feels like your entire future is **in the balance**.*

---

in a situation for which one is not qualified or prepared

*He got **in over** his **head** when he agreed to do all of the paperwork for the project.*

by the book

---

as far as someone **is concerned**

---

in no time

---

by virtue of

---

for the time being

according to the rules or directions; correctly
*There weren't any violations—she did everything **by the book**.*

---

in someone's opinion
*I thought it was great, but **as far as** he **is concerned** it was the worst movie of the year.*

---

very quickly; right away
*The cookies are almost done; they will be ready **in no time**.*

---

because of; on the basis of
*She got the job **by virtue of** her superior language skills.*

---

for now; at this time, but not necessarily in the future
*Let's keep this project a secret **for the time being**.*

by all means

---

by no means

---

as usual

---

back to/at square one

---

in view of

certainly; definitely
*If you go to that restaurant, **by all means**, try the salmon.*

---

absolutely not; not at all
*She is a talented singer but **by no means** the best in the choir.*

---

as ordinarily or habitually happens; like always
*I planned to study before class today, but, **as usual**, I overslept.*

---

back to the point where one started, as if no progress had been made
*If this doesn't work, we can go **back to square one**.*
*Their first plan failed, so now they are **back at square one**.*

---

considering; taking into account
*His writing is especially impressive **in view of** the fact that English is not his first language.*

IDIOM LIST 21

in the long run

---

by the way

---

for the most part

---

as yet

---

in light of

after a long time; in the end; eventually
*It may seem hard to save money for retirement now, but **in the long run** you will be very glad that you did.*

---

incidentally
*I read that book you lent me. **By the way**, did you know that the author lives near here?*

---

in general; mostly
*His grades this year were good, **for the most part**.*

---

up to the present time; as of now
*They will be hiring a new secretary, but **as yet** they have not done so.*

---

considering; because of; taking into account
*She was given a lighter punishment **in light of** the fact that this was the first time she had broken the rules.*

for good measure

---

against all/the odds

---

by hand

---

the looks of

---

on the spot

in addition; beyond what is needed
*The recipe called for four cloves of garlic, but I added two more **for good measure**.*

---

despite it being very unlikely; incredibly, unexpectedly
***Against all odds**, she won her match against the five-time state champion.*
*He recovered from the operation and, **against the odds**, was able to walk again.*

---

without using a machine
*Delicate fabrics like cashmere should be washed **by hand**.*

---

based on the appearance of something; apparently
*From **the looks of** the orientation assembly, there must be fewer students at school this year.*
*The bake sale is raising a lot of money this year, by **the looks of** it.*

---

1. immediately
2. in an awkward position where one is forced to make a difficult decision right away
*1. She didn't expect to get an answer for several weeks, but they accepted her application **on the spot**.*
*2. He put me **on the spot** by proposing marriage in front of his whole family.*

with one voice

---

warts and all

---

as a matter of fact

---

on behalf of

---

as a rule

unanimously; in unison
*The company's employees approved the policy **with one voice**.*

---

including a person's faults as well as his or her positive qualities
*Parents love their children unconditionally, **warts and all**.*

---

actually; in fact
*The outcome of a military conflict is not simply based on casualties; **as a matter of fact**, the Union Army suffered greater losses than the Confederate Army in the American Civil War.*

---

1. in the interest of; in support of
2. as a representative of; in the name of
*1. We are raising money **on behalf of** the local food bank.*
*2. The lawyer wrote a letter **on behalf of** his client, requesting a meeting.*

---

usually; in general
*I don't like documentary films **as a rule**, but this one is extremely interesting.*

one by one

---

on the loose

---

under the weather

---

in the affirmative

---

in the negative

individually; in succession; one at a time
*When your work seems overwhelming, it can be helpful to deal with your
assignments **one by one**, instead of trying to accomplish everything at once.*

out in public
*The community was concerned when they heard that a convict had escaped
from prison and was **on the loose**.*

sick; not feeling well
*She's not coming in to work today, because she's feeling a bit **under the
weather**.*

positive answer; yes
*When he asked the committee if they thought funding the project was a good
idea, they responded **in the affirmative**.*

negative answer; no
*He asked the woman for a date, but she answered **in the negative**.*

EXERCISES

VOCABULARY LIST 1

1. He was able to _____ the outcome without knowing many details.

   a. predict
   b. volunteer
   c. immigrate
   d. violate

2. Because she was a minor, someone had to _____ her on the flight.

   a. relax
   b. volunteer
   c. accompany
   d. restrict

3. He _____ the book with bright colors and geometric patterns.

   a. predicted
   b. relaxed
   c. restricted
   d. illustrated

4. When she went to enter the library, her access card was _____ so she couldn't get in.

   a. denied
   b. approved
   c. accepted
   d. violated

5. He was selected in the drawing, but he couldn't claim the prize because he found out he wasn't _____.

   a. accompanied
   b. eligible
   c. volunteered
   d. denied

VOCABULARY LIST 2

1. The reporter wanted to _____ all of the illegal activity that was going on at the plant.

   a. absorb
   b. expose
   c. unite
   d. purchase

2. The sea animal _____ to the side of the boat even in the rough weather.

   a. united
   b. absorbed
   c. interpreted
   d. adhered

3. When she went to the pound, she was able to _____ the dog she wanted.

   a. revise
   b. influence
   c. interpret
   d. select

4. He studied for seven years to obtain his _____.

   a. demonstration
   b. purchase
   c. degree
   d. influence

5. She found that the best way to teach something new was to _____ it.

   a. adjust
   b. purchase
   c. demonstrate
   d. adjust

377

VOCABULARY LIST 3

1. No one could understand the confusing _____ presented.

   a. paradox
   b. enhance
   c. pedestrian
   d. implement

2. She was very good at _____ others to accomplish their goals.

   a. revealing
   b. motivating
   c. implementing
   d. rejecting

3. There was nothing special about the town, it was very _____.

   a. implemented
   b. responsive
   c. thriving
   d. pedestrian

4. He waited for her to _____ before sending another text message.

   a. respond
   b. accelerate
   c. thrive
   d. implement

5. Out of the two of them, she was always first to _____ a plan.

   a. enhance
   b. strive
   c. formulate
   d. thrive

VOCABULARY LIST 4

1. His teacher _____ a lot of time into tutoring him.

   a. described
   b. modified
   c. investigated
   d. invested

2. She _____ that the bill should be passed.

   a. modified
   b. involved
   c. contended
   d. invested

3. Everyone in the class liked her because she was so _____ and easy to get along with.

   a. amiable
   b. fluent
   c. invested
   d. involved

4. When the reporter questioned him, he _____ to comment.

   a. invested
   b. declined
   c. modified
   d. anticipated

5. Because he did not pass the class, he took it two _____ years in a row.

   a. fluent
   b. invested
   c. modified
   d. consecutive

VOCABULARY LIST 5

Pair the word on the left with its closest match on the right.

Word	Definition
1. participate	A. be involved
2. fiction	B. swap
3. substitute	C. reduce
4. abbreviate	D. stop
5. prevent	E. invented

VOCABULARY LIST 6

Pair the word on the left with its closest match on the right.

Word	Definition
1. acclaim	A. involve
2. cancel	B. observe
3. engage	C. praise
4. inquire	D. stop
5. monitor	E. ask

VOCABULARY LIST 7

Pair the word on the left with its closest match on the right.

Word	Definition
1. approach	A. acceptable
2. decent	B. come toward
3. collect	C. check
4. consult	D. accumulate
5. unify	E. bring together

VOCABULARY LIST 8

1. She completed her portion of the paper and planned to _____ his writings after he sent them to her.
   a. insert
   b. cooperate
   c. dominate
   d. facilitate

2. Each time he spoke on the topic, he was able to _____ an aspect of the subject I hadn't thought of before
   a. facilitate
   b. cooperate
   c. interrupt
   d. illuminate

3. She hated to _____ people while they were talking.
   a. insert
   b. correspond
   c. illuminate
   d. interrupt

4. He was always _____ her on her style.
   a. manipulating
   b. facilitating
   c. complimenting
   d. corresponding

5. He was always on his best behavior because he wanted to keep his spotless _____.
   a. address
   b. consideration
   c. reputation
   d. protection

VOCABULARY LIST 9

Pair the word on the left with its closest match on the right.

Word	Definition
1. expand	A. focus
2. clarify	B. reflect
3. concentrate	C. simplify
4. conscious	D. increase
5. ponder	E. cognizant

VOCABULARY LIST 10

Pair the word on the left with its closest match on the right.

Word	Definition
1. culminate	A. diverge
2. register	B. to end
3. deviate	C. validate
4. succeed	D. comprehend
5. justify	E. prosper

VOCABULARY LIST 11

Pair the word on the left with its closest match on the right.

Word	Definition
1. indicate	A. specify
2. petition	B. delay
3. hesitate	C. to ask for
4. estimate	D. revise
5. edit	E. approximate

VOCABULARY LIST 12

1. Because the roads in his city were rough, she needed a _____ vehicle.

   a. durable
   b. display
   c. promoted
   d. consumed

2. He wanted to _____ all possible issues before they happened.

   a. injure
   b. eliminate
   c. promote
   d. distribute

3. She watched his _____ closely to see if he was bothered by her words.

   a. comparison
   b. depletion
   c. combination
   d. reaction

4. He was nervous to get behind the _____ and give his first speech.

   a. reaction
   b. promotion
   c. podium
   d. elimination

5. She put on so much makeup that even her mother could barely _____ her.

   a. react
   b. recognize
   c. distribute
   d. injure

1. After her exams, she shifted her _____ to her upcoming wedding.

   a. focus
   b. tolerance
   c. identification
   d. persuasion

2. They _____ a study plan to pass the test.

   a. focused
   b. formulated
   c. stored
   d. persuaded

3. Because he was doing what most men would do, his actions _____ the male stereotype.

   a. organized
   b. generated
   c. guaranteed
   d. perpetuated

4. Even though she was a substitute teacher, she _____ her own rules on the students.

   a. guaranteed
   b. imposed
   c. stored
   d. contradicted

5. He _____ all of the important information for the test in his brain.

   a. stored
   b. replaced
   c. networked
   d. contradicted

1. The spectators must remain silent while court is in _____.

   a. valid
   b. session
   c. present
   d. awareness

2. They were told to leave everything _____ inside their hotel room.

   a. valid
   b. equivalent
   c. valuable
   d. subtle

3. When she edited the presentation, the most important aspect to her was _____, so that everything looked the same.

   a. consistency
   b. vagueness
   c. conduct
   d. awareness

4. When he joined the club, he was assigned a _____ to teach him the basics.

   a. preliminary
   b. present
   c. base
   d. mentor

5. Because of her bad grade on the test, the student _____ the class.

   a. mentored
   b. presented
   c. failed
   d. based

VOCABULARY LIST 15

Pair the word on the left with its closest match on the right.

Word	Definition
1. universal	A. optimistic
2. domestic	B. widespread
3. merit	C. good quality
4. explore	D. investigate
5. positive	E. national

VOCABULARY LIST 16

Pair the word on the left with its closest match on the right.

Word	Definition
1. obtain	A. amazing
2. remarkable	B. useful
3. beneficial	C. accessible
4. available	D. procure
5. verify	E. validate

VOCABULARY LIST 17

Pair the word on the left with its closest match on the right.

Word	Definition
1. potential	A. possibility
2. reflect	B. consider
3.phenomenon	C. touching
4. adjacent	D. intricate
5. complex	E. spectacle

VOCABULARY LIST 18

1. She had taken the entry level class, so she was already _____ with most of the basic concepts.

   a. familiar
   b. compatible
   c. sufficient
   d. coherent

2. The rules were so _____ that no one knew whether or not they were allowed to ask for outside help.

   a. profound
   b. ambiguous
   c. minuscule
   d. compatible

3. No one will decide your future for you; you must take the _____ to do so yourself.

   a. ambiguous
   b. intensity
   c. complications
   d. initiative

4. His difficult request seemed to _____ the matter even further.

   a. adequate
   b. profound
   c. complicate
   d. automatic

5. Although the hostel was not amazing, it was _____ for their overnight stay.

   a. adequate
   b. conceivable
   c. medical
   d. automatic

1. She performed _____ review of the material before the test to ensure she was fully prepared.
   a. an objective
   b. a comprehensive
   c. a minimum
   d. a temporary

2. Thus, she spent _____ amount of time studying.
   a. an inevitable
   b. a contrary
   c. an ethnic
   d. a considerable

3. She was ecstatic because her grade on the test was _____.
   a. outstanding
   b. legal
   c. previous
   d. minimum

4. He _____ his paper two weeks before the deadline.
   a. contradicted
   b. submitted
   c. considered
   d. temped

5. In order to determine if he was a good candidate and didn't have anything in his past that he was trying to hide, they asked him many questions relating to his _____.
   a. source
   b. minimum
   c. background
   d. temporary

1. Signing a waiver was _____ before attending the tour of the plant.
   a. mandatory
   b. incredible
   c. brief
   d. predominant

2. It didn't matter how long he was gone, she always remained _____.
   a. strict
   b. mediocre
   c. loyal
   d. mutual

3. Their respect was _____, they both looked up to each other.
   a. random
   b. mutual
   c. global
   d. mediocre

4. While her mother often let her do as she pleased, her father was far more _____.
   a. global
   b. mediocre
   c. loyal
   d. strict

5. The environment was very important to him, so he did his best to _____ water any chance he got.
   a. conserve
   b. prepare
   c. appropriate
   d. liable

VOCABULARY LIST 21

1. They conducted interviews for months to find the best _____ for the assistant position.
   a. publication
   b. candidate
   c. phase
   d. commerce

2. After she saw the _____ in her report, she rushed to fix it before the presentation.
   a. error
   b. behavior
   c. prerequisite
   d. method

3. Before you present information to a group, you must verify that the _____ of that information is reliable.
   a. error
   b. behavior
   c. method
   d. source

4. It is important to be _____ when setting expectations for a project so that the requirements are completed on time.
   a. revolutionary
   b. realistic
   c. wise
   d. innovative

5. His letter demanded a _____ response.
   a. prompt
   b. source
   c. method
   d. behavior

VOCABULARY LIST 22

1. He liked to remain calm and consider his reactions carefully so that he never ended up in the middle of _____.
   a. an opportunity
   b. a concept
   c. a controversy
   d. an alternative

2. She studied until she became completely _____ in the subject.
   a. resourceful
   b. instance
   c. proficient
   d. conceptualized

3. He was so busy that he did not have time to complete the _____ assignment.
   a. tedious
   b. proof
   c. resourceful
   d. controversial

4. She often ignored him whenever he _____ her.
   a. cautioned
   b. proved
   c. diversified
   d. conceptualized

5. He always needed before he would believe anything.
   a. collaboration
   b. proof
   c. opportunity
   d. diversity

VOCABULARY LIST 23

1. She wasn't sure why she felt so happy, but she was glad her _____ had improved over how she had felt the day before.

   a. attitude
   b. level
   c. comment
   d. strategy

2. He always liked to figure out his _____ before starting a game.

   a. strategy
   b. generation
   c. tradition
   d. comment

3. She tried her best to listen to the _____, but the material was so boring she almost fell asleep.

   a. circumstance
   b. generation
   c. function
   d. lecture

4. It is easiest to play shuffleboard if the surface is _____.

   a. function
   b. lecture
   c. level
   d. circumstance

5. She regularly performed _____ on the different species of plants in the lab.

   a. an analysis
   b. an emphasis
   c. an era
   d. a tradition

VOCABULARY LIST 24

1. The _____ did not change no matter who was enforcing it.

   a. boon
   b. overall
   c. policy
   d. unison

2. She was very well prepared; _____, the presentation was flawless.

   a. nevertheless
   b. consequently
   c. chiefly
   d. recently

3. There is no doubt about it: he _____ wants to go on vacation.

   a. furthermore
   b. thereby
   c. initially
   d. definitely

4. She was often complemented on the _____ of her hair, since it extended well down the middle of her back.

   a. period
   b. initial
   c. length
   d. policy

5. Many dinosaurs lived in the Jurassic _____.

   a. period
   b. policy
   c. length
   d. initial

VOCABULARY LIST 25

Match the word on the left to its closest match on the right.

Word	Definition
1. expert	A. stop
2. disrupt	B. facts
3. data	C. viewpoint
4. perspective	D. investigate
5. experiment	E. adept

VOCABULARY LIST 26

Pair the word on the left with its closest match on the right.

Word	Definition
1. appearance	A. look
2. individual	B. separate
3. supervise	C. omission
4. exception	D. look after
5. anxious	E. stressed

IDIOM LIST 1

1. He found testing the limits fun, so he was always _____.

    a. following suit
    b. pushing the envelope
    c. abiding by the rules
    d. backing something up

2. There is no telling what will happen; we will have to wait to see how it all _____.

    a. pans out
    b. accounts for
    c. gives away
    d. backs up

3. Since she is new to the organization, she is looking for someone who _____ to help her learn.

    a. had second thoughts
    b. accounted for
    c. panned out
    d. knows the ropes

4. In high school, I spent all of my afternoons _____ my siblings.

    a. backing up
    b. looking forward to
    c. looking after
    d. looking into

5. I spend each weekday _____ to the weekend.

    a. testing the waters
    b. looking after
    c. looking into
    d. looking forward to

IDIOM LIST 2

1. I never knew he was lying at first, but I finally _____.

    a. touched base
    b. reined him in
    c. saw the light
    d. looked up to him

2. My sister always trusted her and gave her _____.

    a. his own
    b. the benefit of the doubt
    c. saw the light
    d. the information

3. He normally spoke his mind, but today he was careful to _____.

    a. touch base
    b. see the light
    c. off base
    d. hold his tongue

4. She had a meeting with her supervisor to discuss false allegations and _____.

    a. use up
    b. set the record straight
    c. off base
    d. see the light

5. Whenever he went into a match, he made sure to _____ to see what he was up against.

    a. size up the competition
    b. see the light
    c. look up to
    d. off base

IDIOM LIST 3

1. After he was unemployed for six months, people told him to _____ in his job selection.

   a. cross paths
   b. run into
   c. lower the bar
   d. end up

2. I don't want to punish you, but _____.

   a. I've crossed paths
   b. my hands are tied
   c. I run into
   d. I see things

3. When she didn't see him for two weeks, she _____ often.

   a. went through with it
   b. asked after him
   c. ended up
   d. got his act together

4. Even though I am confident that I can handle the large project, I know I _____.

   a. have my work cut out for me
   b. crossed paths
   c. will run into
   d. will end up

5. The police _____ in their investigation.

   a. cut out
   b. ended up
   c. run into
   d. left no stone unturned

IDIOM LIST 4

1. Her visits were never planned; she was always _____ unannounced.

   a. going wrong
   b. erring on the side of caution
   c. on the dot
   d. dropping in

2. Now that he is working and has two children, _____ and we don't see him often.

   a. he is going wrong
   b. he is on the dot
   c. his hands are full
   d. on occasion

3. She didn't want to rush the project, so she made sure to _____.

   a. on occasion
   b. go back to the drawing board
   c. go wrong
   d. take her time

4. Even though they didn't always _____ they enjoyed working together.

   a. go back to the drawing board
   b. go wrong
   c. see eye to eye
   d. on the dot

5. He was accepted to five different schools and was having trouble _____ the list.

   a. erring on the side of caution
   b. narrowing down
   c. going wrong
   d. erring on the side of

IDIOM LIST 5

1. The task at hand was difficult, but she was not willing to _____.

    a. take someone's place
    b. throw in the towel
    c. stay out of
    d. wear thin

2. The mistake was caused by an error on his part, but his coworkers did not want to _____ so they all took the blame together.

    a. throw him to the wolves
    b. stay out of
    c. wear thin
    d. carry out

3. She never wanted to offend anyone, so she did her best to _____ every argument.

    a. carry out
    b. stay out of
    c. take someone's place
    d. wear thin

4. He was normally so understanding, but these days _____.

    a. he stayed out
    b. he took someone's place
    c. he carried out
    d. his patience was wearing thin

5. She didn't want anyone at work to notice her, so she _____.

    a. wore thin
    b. took someone's place
    c. kept a low profile
    d. carried out

IDIOM LIST 6

1. It was important that everyone understood what was being said, so she made sure to _____.

    a. think better of it
    b. draw the line
    c. slap her wrist
    d. get the message across

2. I was always so sure, but recently he _____ on my beliefs.

    a. cast doubt
    b. thought better of it
    c. drew the line
    d. slapped a wrist

3. Her children were her priority, so she _____ to spend as much time with them as she could.

    a. kept an eye
    b. made do
    c. made sense
    d. made a point

4. He worked the entire day, refusing to _____.

    a. have a piece of cake
    b. draw the line
    c. take a break
    d. think better of it

5. She was going to call in sick, but realizing her boss would punish her for lying, she _____.

    a. gave him a slap on the wrist
    b. had a piece of cake
    c. drew the line
    d. thought better of it

IDIOM LIST 7

1. He never gave up; he always _____ his task.

   a. stood out
   b. got the best of
   c. wound up
   d. kept at

2. If we keep driving this way there is no telling where we'll _____.

   a. keep up
   b. wind up
   c. get the best
   d. jump on the bandwagon

3. She wanted to know who ate the cookies; she was determined to _____.

   a. jump on the bandwagon
   b. get rid
   c. get to the bottom of it
   d. get the best

4. Even though the shirt had holes in it, he refused to _____ of it.

   a. get the best
   b. jump on the bandwagon
   c. get to the bottom
   d. get rid

5. Before you go on the trip, you should _____ about your finances.

   a. think twice
   b. get the best
   c. jump on the bandwagon
   d. wind down

IDIOM LIST 8

1. She was a free spirit, but her parents always _____ doing things.

   a. sat around
   b. hit the books
   c. hit the nail on the head
   d. kept her from

2. He told the kids to _____ in the office while he went to speak to their teacher.

   a. split hairs
   b. sit tight
   c. show up
   d. hit the nail on the head

3. Before she made any judgments, she was sure to _____.

   a. take all of the information into account
   b. sit tight
   c. show up
   d. split hairs

4. I warned him to be home on time, but I know that _____.

   a. will split hairs
   b. he hit the nail on the head
   c. goes without saying
   d. he hit the books

5. She was so tired that she decided to _____ early tonight.

   a. split hairs
   b. hit the hay
   c. hit the nail on the head
   d. lend a hand

IDIOM LIST 9

1. She had made a mistake, so she went to the website and wrote an apology in an effort to _____.
   a. off the record
   b. count on
   c. on the fence
   d. save face

2. He was up next for a promotion as soon as his boss retired, so he was just _____.
   a. keeping track
   b. off the hook
   c. biding his time
   d. fielding questions

3. She was the first to hold the role in the company; thus, she _____ others in the future.
   a. counted as
   b. paved the way for
   c. counted on
   d. saved her breath for

4. After he broke his leg, the doctor told him to _____ for a while.
   a. take it easy
   b. off the hook
   c. count on
   d. off the record

5. She is always so reliable that I know I can _____ to come through.
   a. off the record
   b. off the hook
   c. pin down the details
   d. count on her

IDIOM LIST 10

1. They expected him to complete the project sufficiently, but he _____ their expectations.
   a. fell short of
   b. let on
   c. put off
   d. passed up

2. Everything in her life was going perfectly and _____.
   a. putting off
   b. falling into place
   c. letting on
   d. passing up

3. The project was _____ nicely.
   a. letting on
   b. icing on the cake
   c. coming along
   d. falling short

4. I don't have time for a long explanation; just _____.
   a. pass up
   b. let on
   c. cut off
   d. cut to the chase

5. He _____ before I could finish.
   a. cut to the chase
   b. cut me off
   c. let on
   d. took its toll

IDIOM LIST 11

1. She thought that the fire started in the bedroom, but the firefighters _____ that possibility.

    a. gut feeling
    b. ruled out
    c. played it safe
    d. played with fire

2. She was never careless; she always _____.

    a. played with fire
    b. played it safe
    c. turned a blind eye
    d. put down roots

3. I asked him to _____ for any new position that may come available.

    a. keep me in mind
    b. turn a blind eye
    c. bring me up to date
    d. put down roots

4. He wanted to _____ his father's company one day.

    a. rule out
    b. cry wolf
    c. take over
    d. put down roots

5. Don't _____; just tell me exactly what happened.

    a. bring me up to date
    b. put down roots
    c. beat around the bush
    d. rule out

IDIOM LIST 12

1. He did not want to _____ in their activities.

    a. tie the knot
    b. put the ball in his court
    c. take part
    d. above board

2. You committed the offense; now you have _____.

    a. above board
    b. to tie the knot
    c. third time's a charm
    d. to pay the price

3. I am impartial; I am not one to _____ in an argument.

    a. put the cart before the horse
    b. be on even keel
    c. be above board
    d. take sides

4. She held three different jobs and was always _____.

    a. wearing different hats
    b. third time's a charm
    c. tying the knot
    d. above board

5. She always had a way of catching me _____ when I least expected it.

    a. third time's a charm
    b. off guard
    c. even keel
    d. above board

IDIOM LIST 13

1. He was quick to _____
   so that he did not waste any
   time.

   a. run of the mill
   b. get to the point
   c. white collar
   d. blue collar

2. I usually have so much to say,
   but when I won the award I
   was _____.

   a. at a loss for words
   b. best of both worlds
   c. full-fledged
   d. run of the mill

3. She always tried to help
   anyone who was feeling
   _____.

   a. to the point
   b. on the tip of their tongue
   c. down and out
   d. beside the point

4. We entered into an agreement
   that was so beneficial, it
   was really a _____
   situation for both parties.

   a. beside the point
   b. run of the mill
   c. no-win
   d. win-win

5. After her promotion, she
   was _____ her old
   coworkers.

   a. in charge of
   b. best of both worlds
   c. full-fledged
   d. white collar to

IDIOM LIST 14

1. Her supervisor let her know
   that she was _____
   and should keep heading in
   the direction she was headed.

   a. in touch
   b. on the fence
   c. on the wrong track
   d. on the right track

2. He was so _____ in his
   work that he lost track of time.

   a. in the wings
   b. wrapped up
   c. on the fence
   d. in touch

3. When he failed out of school,
   his parents thought he was
   _____ for his future.

   a. on the same page
   b. on the fence
   c. on the right track
   d. on the wrong track

4. I am glad that my project
   manager and I are always
   _____, because it
   makes it really easy to work
   with her.

   a. at a premium
   b. in the wings
   c. on the same page
   d. in the pipeline

5. When she moved away,
   he made sure to stay
   _____ with her.

   a. in touch
   b. in wings
   c. in the pipeline
   d. in line

IDIOM LIST 15

1. Even though he was normally a man _____, tonight he had a lot to say.

   a. at the mercy
   b. of few words
   c. fine tuning
   d. on top of

2. I wanted to take on the new project, but the supervisor told me it was _____.

   a. out of the question
   b. on top of
   c. letting the cat out of the bag
   d. fine tuning

3. Our company is _____ of the competition.

   a. once in a blue moon
   b. cutting the corners
   c. light years ahead
   d. easy as pie

4. They tried not to let the argument get _____ because they did not want to draw attention to themselves.

   a. at the mercy of
   b. cutting corners
   c. once in a blue moon
   d. out of hand

5. I was surprised to get his letter, since I received mail from him only _____.

   a. on top of
   b. once in a blue moon
   c. easy as pie
   d. cutting corners

IDIOM LIST 16

1. The garage sale was full of _____ and didn't seem to have a complete set of anything.

   a. second wind
   b. mixed emotions
   c. powers that be
   d. odds and ends

2. He wanted to be sure there was _____ before the game commenced.

   a. a last minute
   b. a level playing field
   c. powers that be
   d. mixed emotions

3. She normally kept her opinions to herself, but his outburst was _____, and she finally said something to him.

   a. last minute
   b. second wind
   c. the last straw
   d. mixed emotions

4. He didn't think it was harmful to tell _____, but she didn't appreciate any kind of falsehood.

   a. the light at the end of the tunnel
   b. white lies
   c. last minute
   d. red tape

5. She got along with most new people right away because she was great at _____.

   a. second wind
   b. last minute
   c. mixed emotions
   d. small talk

IDIOM LIST 17

1. Hurry! There is _____!
   a. an upper hand
   b. a clean slate
   c. no time to lose
   d. face value

2. You need to figure out the _____ before you begin the project.
   a. cutting edge
   b. bitter pill
   c. face value
   d. game plan

3. The company was always far advanced above the competition and on the _____.
   a. double-edged sword
   b. zero tolerance
   c. clean slate
   d. cutting edge

4. She was tired during the day so she drank coffee, but she couldn't fall asleep at night because she drank coffee. It was a _____.
   a. vicious cycle
   b. clean slate
   c. face value
   d. zero tolerance

5. He never cared about anyone's past; he always liked to start out friendships with a _____.
   a. Achilles' heel
   b. clean slate
   c. zero tolerance
   d. double-edged sword

IDIOM LIST 18

1. Even though we got into a disagreement, there were no _____ afterwards.
   a. ivory towers
   b. hard feelings
   c. recipes for disaster
   d. big pictures

2. When someone is in a rough situation you will often see their _____.
   a. true colors
   b. ivory tower
   c. bells and whistles
   d. salad days

3. After their disagreement, he apologized and offered an _____.
   a. olive branch
   b. ill-gotten gain
   c. ivory tower
   d. across the board

4. They won the lawsuit but lost their good reputation, so it was a _____.
   a. bell and whistle
   b. big picture
   c. recipe for disaster
   d. Pyrrhic victory

5. The new facility was _____.
   a. salad days
   b. the big picture
   c. the state of the art
   d. at odds

1. I don't see her frequently, only every _____.
   a. at stake
   b. on and off
   c. now and then
   d. be that as it may

2. I hadn't heard from him in years and he suddenly called _____.
   a. ahead of time
   b. to speak of
   c. out of the blue
   d. under the table

3. Her policies went _____ with her world views.
   a. hand in hand
   b. on and off
   c. be that as it may
   d. at stake

4. The future is unclear; you never know what will happen _____.
   a. down the road
   b. on her behalf
   c. at stake
   d. to speak of

5. His secretary answered all emails _____.
   a. to speak of
   b. on his behalf
   c. at stake
   d. be that as it may

1. You never know what will happen _____, so you need to do your best at all times.
   a. by the book
   b. by all means
   c. over someone's head
   d. down the line

2. She was never one to _____; she said everything to your face.
   a. by all means
   b. back to square one
   c. talk behind someone's back
   d. over someone's head

3. He was absolutely convinced he was right _____.
   a. by no means
   b. beyond the shadow of a doubt
   c. over his head
   d. in view of

4. _____, she is innocent; I don't care what the reporters say.
   a. As far as I am concerned
   b. Back to square one
   c. In view of
   d. By virtue of

5. I thought it would take a while for the car repairs to be completed, but they were done _____.
   a. by the book
   b. for the time being
   c. as usual
   d. in no time

IDIOM LIST 21

1. _____, I did get a
   haircut; thank you for noticing.

   a. As a matter of fact
   b. In light of
   c. As a rule
   d. On the spot

2. Even though she was
   completely out of shape, she
   won the race _____.

   a. in light of
   b. with one voice
   c. against all odds
   d. by hand

3. _____ the entire city,
   I would like to award you this
   medal of recognition.

   a. With one voice
   b. As yet
   c. In light of
   d. On behalf of

4. He didn't go to work today
   because he was feeling

   _____.

   a. under the weather
   b. by hand
   c. as a rule
   d. on the spot

5. The tiger escaped from the zoo
   and now it is _____ in
   the city.

   a. by hand
   b. on the loose
   c. on the spot
   d. with one voice

ANSWERS

VOCABULARY LIST 1
1. A
2. C
3. D
4. A
5. B

VOCABULARY LIST 2
1. B
2. D
3. D
4. C
5. C

VOCABULARY LIST 3
1. A
2. B
3. D
4. A
5. C

VOCABULARY LIST 4
1. D
2. C
3. A
4. B
5. D

VOCABULARY LIST 5
1. A
2. E
3. B
4. C
5. D

VOCABULARY LIST 6
1. C
2. D
3. A
4. E
5. B

VOCABULARY LIST 7
1. B
2. A
3. D
4. C
5. E

VOCABULARY LIST 8
1. A
2. D
3. D
4. C
5. C

VOCABULARY LIST 9
1. D
2. C
3. A
4. E
5. B

VOCABULARY LIST 10
1. B
2. D
3. A
4. E
5. C

VOCABULARY LIST 11
1. A
2. C
3. B
4. E
5. D

VOCABULARY LIST 12
1. A
2. B
3. D
4. C
5. B

VOCABULARY LIST 13
1. A
2. B
3. D
4. B
5. A

VOCABULARY LIST 14
1. B
2. C
3. A
4. D
5. C

VOCABULARY LIST 15
1. B
2. E
3. C
4. D
5. A

VOCABULARY LIST 16
1. D
2. A
3. B
4. C
5. E

VOCABULARY LIST 17
1. A
2. B
3. E
4. C
5. D

VOCABULARY LIST 18
1. A
2. B
3. D
4. C
5. A

VOCABULARY LIST 19
1. B
2. D
3. A
4. B
5. C

VOCABULARY LIST 20
1. A
2. C
3. B
4. D
5. A

VOCABULARY LIST 21
1. B
2. A
3. D
4. B
5. A

VOCABULARY LIST 22
1. C
2. C
3. A
4. A
5. B

VOCABULARY LIST 23
1. A
2. A
3. D
4. C
5. A

VOCABULARY LIST 24
1. C
2. B
3. D
4. C
5. A

VOCABULARY LIST 25

1. E
2. A
3. B
4. C
5. D

VOCABULARY LIST 26

1. A
2. B
3. D
4. C
5. E

IDIOM LIST 1

1. B
2. A
3. D
4. C
5. D

IDIOM LIST 2

1. C
2. B
3. D
4. B
5. A

IDIOM LIST 3

1. C
2. B
3. B
4. A
5. D

IDIOM LIST 4

1. D
2. C
3. D
4. C
5. B

IDIOM LIST 5

1. B
2. A
3. B
4. D
5. C

IDIOM LIST 6

1. D
2. A
3. D
4. C
5. D

IDIOM LIST 7

1. D
2. B
3. C
4. D
5. A

IDIOM LIST 8

1. D
2. B
3. A
4. C
5. B

IDIOM LIST 9

1. D
2. C
3. B
4. A
5. D

IDIOM LIST 10

1. A
2. B
3. C
4. D
5. B

IDIOM LIST 11
1. B
2. B
3. A
4. C
5. C

IDIOM LIST 12
1. C
2. D
3. D
4. A
5. B

IDIOM LIST 13
1. B
2. A
3. C
4. D
5. A

IDIOM LIST 14
1. D
2. B
3. D
4. C
5. A

IDIOM LIST 15
1. B
2. A
3. C
4. D
5. B

IDIOM LIST 16
1. D
2. B
3. C
4. B
5. D

IDIOM LIST 17
1. C
2. D
3. D
4. A
5. B

IDIOM LIST 18
1. B
2. A
3. A
4. D
5. C

IDIOM LIST 19
1. C
2. C
3. A
4. A
5. B

IDIOM LIST 20
1. D
2. C
3. B
4. A
5. D

IDIOM LIST 21
1. A
2. C
3. D
4. A
5. B